D1057947

THE PRESENCE

ALSO BY BRUCE LARSON

A Call to Holy Living
Faith for the Journey
My Creator, My Friend
Wind and Fire
Communicator's Commentary: Luke
Believe and Belong
There's a Lot More to Health Than Not Being Sick
Dare to Live Now
Living on the Growing Edge
No Longer Strangers
The One and Only You
Thirty Days to a New You
Risky Christianity
The Meaning and Mystery of Being Human
Setting Men Free
The Emerging Church
Ask Me to Dance

With J. Keith Miller:

The Edge of Adventure
Living the Adventure
The Passionate People: Carriers of the Spirit

the PRESENCE

the God who delivers and guides

Bruce Larson

Harper & Row, Publishers, San Francisco

Cambridge, Hagerstown, New York, Philadelphia, Washington
London, Mexico City, São Paulo, Singapore, Sydney

 For information address Harper & Row, Publishers, Inc., 10 East 53rd Street, New York, N.Y. 10022. Published simultaneously in Canada by Fitzhenry & Whiteside Limited, Toronto.

FIRST EDITION

Library of Congress Cataloging-in-Publication Data

Larson, Bruce.

The Presence : the God who delivers and guides.

1. Bible. O.T. Exodus—Sermons. 2. Ten commandments—Sermons. 3. Presbyterian Church (U.S.A.)—Sermons. 4. Presbyterian Church—Sermons. 5. Sermons, American. I. Title.

BS1245.4.L34 1988 222'.1206 87-46214

ISBN 0-06-064933-1

---

88 89 90 91 92 RRD 10 9 8 7 6 5 4 3 2 1

To Benjamin, Luke, and Timothy
Children of our children and children of God

Contents

Prologue

What do we know about God—for sure? Who is He? What is He really like? If we believe the Bible, there are two things about His nature that we can be certain of: God is our Father and God is love.

Now those are descriptions that I can understand. I am a father and, though my love for my children is imperfect and far from unconditional, I know what love feels like and what love does.

When my children were young and still living under my roof, I often had to rescue them. Love does that—and loses count of the times. I can remember trips to the principal's office to retrieve a troublemaker. I can remember trips to the emergency room at the hospital. I can remember trips to appease angry neighbors. I can remember trips to recover a banged-up car. I can remember trips to confront teachers who seemed to be persecuting my children. I can even remember a trip to the police station to pick up a wayward teenager. A loving parent delivers his or her children from the perils of life—whether they are in trouble they deserve and helped to create, or whether they are victims of an unfeeling and corrupt society. Love delivers, when possible.

But a loving parent also tries to help those same children learn how to avoid catastrophy and pain and self-inflicted destruction. By teaching and warning and instructing, a parent attempts to guide the child around life's pitfalls. "Do this and you will prosper." "Don't do those things that are sure to unleash unimaginable pain on yourself and many others." Love warns, love instructs. And when advice is not taken, love suffers with and then, one more time, tries to deliver.

Exodus is perhaps the best Old Testament description of God as the nurturing parent, and this book, based on that story of deliverance, seemed to divide itself very naturally into three parts. Part one deals with God's active deliverance of His people from all sorts of situations. In some cases, they are innocent victims of circumstances. At other times, their trials are of their own making—the result of their willfulness, unbelief, and downright disobedience. Part two explores the Ten Commandments, God's instructions for living a whole, rich, and blessed life. In a sense, this portion is the culmination of this dramatic tale of deliverance. It is God's blueprint for what life in the Kingdom is to be—a single-minded pursuit of His righteousness, characterized by love and charity toward all. The law provides channel markers for your life and mine, those guidelines that bring us safely home.

Part three touches briefly on an age-old question: Where is God when you need Him? He is now, as He was for the wandering Israelites, our invisible deliverer. In our journey through the wilderness, he supplies us with food, water, camels, and resting places. But none of these things are intended to provide ultimate security and satisfaction. No oasis is permanent. It is not just deliverance we seek, but the Deliverer. I hope you'll meet him in new and fresh ways in these pages.

By way of conclusion, let me acknowledge here those people who have helped make this book a reality. First of all, there is that faithful, obedient congregation who live love and live it at high risk—my present family in Christ, the University Presbyterian Church in Seattle. Without their eagerness to hear and do God's word today, there would have been no reason to preach the sermons from which this book comes.

Next, there is my friend and teammate, Hal Jaenson, who transcribed my sermons during the midnight hours at his home. My faithful and enormously gifted administrative assistant, Gretha Osterberg—again in the wee hours—typed, edited, and encouraged.

But the person most essential to the publishing of this book is my wife, life partner, and best friend, Hazel. A gifted writer and editor, she has literally written and rewritten much of the manuscript. She should be listed as the coauthor on the title page, but refuses. It is enough that you, the reader, know.

Bon voyage on your spiritual journey through the wildernesses of life.

I. GOD THE RESCUER

1. No Safe Place

Life is either a celebration of deliverance or an ode to regret. I experienced deliverance for the first time when I encountered the capacity for evil in my own heart. I was an infantry sergeant in World War II. My outfit, the 100th Infantry Division, had helped bring the final victory over Germany and now we were the occupying troops. Life in a ravaged and conquered country is a matter of basic survival, and most personal values have a price tag. There was almost nothing or no one that could not be bought for food, especially coffee or chocolate. American soldiers had these in abundance and, with cynical self-interest and appalling indifference, we made use of them.

My awareness of human depravity, venal behavior, greed, lewdness, moral decay, and rampant materialism was heightened to the breaking point by the realization that I was not just an innocent bystander. I was a participant in, contributor to, and creator of those evil conditions.

At the same time, I considered myself a Christian. I grew up in a great evangelical church in Chicago. My mother was a model of godly zeal. My father was a deacon in the church. I cannot remember a time when I did not believe in the triune God: Father, Son, and Spirit, though I had little experience of Him. I accepted without question all the basic Christian doctrines—the Incarnation, the Atonement, the Resurrection, and fully expected eventually to land in heaven.

But these beliefs had no impact on the way I lived. It was not until I came face to face with my own moral decay as a part of an occupying army that I first cried out to the Lord for deliverance. It happened one dark night in Stuttgart, Germany, while I was guarding a bombed-out ball-bearing factory. Why this nearly demolished building needed guarding, I'll never know, but I thank God for whoever placed me there that particular night. The moon was visible through the charred rafters overhead. I was alone. I took my carbine off my shoulder, ground out my cigarette, kneeled down, and asked the Lord to change me if He could.

I wanted deliverance. I was sick unto death of this arena where human beings preyed upon each other, and I wanted to cease being a participant in it all. I knew I couldn't promise the Lord that I would change, even though I wished with all my heart I could. I had tried that before and failed. Instead, I asked for deliverance. Deliverance from myself. Deliverance from conforming to the depravity around me.

Well, God gave me deliverance. It came in strange ways and shapes. Coincidences, unusual circumstances, a mysterious inner power, and a new set of buddies who were also being delivered. A miracle.

Many decades have passed since then, but I'm more than ever aware that God is always a deliverer—the Deliverer. The Old Testament centers around His ability to deliver His people. The New Testament proclaims the coming of the Savior—the one who saves and delivers all who believe in Him. The name "Jesus" comes from the Hebrew word for "deliverer."

Deliverance takes many forms. God can deliver us from our weakness, from our evil intentions, and from our ignorance. He delivers us from the destruction brought about by our own stupidity and blindness, as well as from those final destructions called death and hell. But this never-ending relationship with God as the deliverer begins when we first look within and behold what manner of being we are.

Perhaps author G. K. Chesterton summed it up best in these words from his story "The Secret of Father Brown."

> No man's really any good 'til he knows how bad he is, or might be; 'til he's realized exactly how much right he has to all this snobbery and sneering, and talking about "criminals" as if they were apes in a forest ten thousand miles away; 'til he's got rid of all the dirty self-deception of talking about low types and deficient skulls; 'til he's squeezed out of his soul the last drop of the oil of Pharisee; 'til his only hope is

somehow or other to have captured one criminal, and kept him safe and sane under his own hat.

Deliverance, personal and corporate, is the theme of the book of Exodus, the second Old Testament book. In these next chapters we will explore the meaning and mode of that deliverance and its relevance for you and me.

The Exodus of the Israelites from Egypt is the central event of the Old Testament in the way that Christ's death and resurrection are the central events of the New Testament. Jews today may be divided theologically and politically, but they are united in the observance and celebration of the Exodus and God's deliverance of their nation. The New Testament is rooted and grounded in the concept of God as He is revealed in the story of the Exodus and in the God of the Ten Commandments, which were subsequently delivered to Moses.

The date of the departure from Egypt is uncertain, according to scholars; it might have occurred in 1589 B.C. or 1220 B.C., or somewhere in between. But there's nothing uncertain about the message of the Book of Exodus. God is active in the affairs of His people. God is not an absent landlord; the Creator intervenes actively in the lives of His people.

Some parallels between the events in Exodus and those recorded in the Gospels may or may not have hidden meaning:

- The Jews spent forty years in the wilderness.
- Jesus began His ministry by praying for forty days in the wilderness.

- The law was given on Mount Sinai.
- A mountain was the scene of Jesus' famous sermon.

- Pharaoh set out to kill all the male Jewish infants.
- King Herod did the same at the time of Jesus' birth.

- There were twelve tribes of Israel.
- Twelve disciples were chosen by Jesus.

- The serpent, the bronze caduceus of modern medicine, was lifted up by Moses to heal those bitten by snakes.
- Jesus said, "But I, when I am lifted up from the earth, will draw all men to myself" (John 12:32).

- The Passover lamb was slain and its blood sprinkled over the doorpost to ensure that the Angel of Death would pass over the Jewish households, killing only the Egyptians.
- When Jesus came to be baptized in the Jordan, John greeted Him with these words, "Look the Lamb of God who takes away the sin of the world" (John 1:29). The Passover was being celebrated by Jesus and His disciples when He instigated the first communion service, a holy sacrament of the Christian church.

- God provided manna day by day in a barren desert, and for forty years the Israelites survived on this hoarfrost kind of food.
- Jesus said, "I am the bread of life. He who comes to me will never go hungry" (John 6:35). He fed the crowd of five thousand which had travelled out to the hills of Galilee to hear His teachings with just seven loaves of bread and a few small fish.

- Moses brought forth water from a rock when the wanderers were thirsty.
- Jesus told the Samaritan woman at the well, "Whoever drinks the water I give him will never thirst. Indeed, the water I give him will become in him a spring of water welling up to eternal life" (John 4:14).

- God appeared to Moses in a burning bush.
- The coming of the Holy Spirit at Pentecost was accompanied by fire.

The parallels are intriguing, to say the least.

But, for our purposes, perhaps the most important parallel is found in the fact that this second book in the Old Testament is the record of an event: God did something. The New Testament also is the proclamation of an event: the coming of a Messiah, the Savior, the Reconciler. Both the Old and New Testaments center in an active, incarnate God at work in the world. Ours is an event-centered faith, rather than an abstract, conceptual faith.

The story of deliverance has its roots, of course, in the events found earlier at the end of the book of Genesis. Joseph, Pharaoh's chief executive officer, arranged to have his father and brothers emigrate to Egypt to escape a drought and its accompanying famine. Present-day Israel, apart from extensive irrigation, is a dry, barren land, even in the best of times. We can imagine the reaction of Jacob and his sons as they moved to the lush, fertile Nile Valley. It would be like a drought and famine victim from today's Ethiopia coming to my home in Seattle, Washington, which is lush and green and surrounded by water. They were delivered from death and brought to Eden, but Eden was, in subsequent years, to become uninhabitable.

The Exodus story begins about four hundred years after that initial emigration and the special status of the Jews is no more. We read that they are unremembered by the new Pharaoh. Some of us have experienced that situation on a personal level. It's a familiar problem for employees caught in the middle of a corporate takeover. Your firm changes hands, new management comes in, and all your hard work and long hours count for nothing. You're unremembered. After four hundred years, the new Pharaoh was taking a hard line. By that time, there were perhaps three million Hebrews in Egypt—and three million aliens could become a dangerous force.

Pharaoh's first plan was to use them to provide labor for public works. For the price of a meal, he conscripted millions of people to build pyramids, storehouses, and all sorts of projects. But even with that kind of persecution, the Hebrews prospered. The next plan was more radical. Pharaoh instructed the midwives to kill all the Jewish males at birth. They were simply to put a thumb over the breathing pipe and announce that the child was stillborn.

We could wonder why he did not just kill them outright. Why did he devise this devious, secret plan? I would guess that, like so many public officials, he wanted to save face. It was a covert operation, if you will. But in these midwives, this most powerful man in the world met his match. Some of these women, we are told, feared God. One or two or three of us who fear God are a force to be reckoned with. The midwives lied and Pharaoh's plan was defeated.

The next scheme was slightly more subtle. The Nile was considered the greatest of all the Egyptian gods, the source of all vegetation and life. Each year on schedule its banks overflowed, bringing fertility to the land. Pharaoh proposed to put the Hebrew baby boys into the Nile and see what disposition this god would make of them. As it has before and since, religion was being used to excuse our inhumanity to our fellow human beings.

After four hundred years, Egypt was no longer an oasis of deliverance for the Israelites, but a place of death, and here is a lesson applicable to all of us. There is no safe place. God does deliver us, as He did the Israelites, but we cannot remain forever at that place of deliverance. Eventually, there is only death.

A friend shared a story with me recently that prompted a whole new train of thought about deliverance. Rick is an avid eagle-watcher. On vacations, he usually takes his family to remote places where the great American bald eagle still rules. On his most recent trip, he witnessed a strange incident. He was sitting on his accustomed rock, high on a ledge overlooking a valley bounded by the kind of rugged cliffs eagles love. He had his notebook on his lap and his binoculars fixed on a large old eagle he had given the name "Boss" because he seemed to be the biggest bird in the valley. Boss was doing lazy rolls, catching the thermals and wheeling effortlessly in the sun.

Suddenly, the bird dove straight down, his eye on a target invisible to my friend. But when he reached the floor of the valley and began to ascend once more, it was obvious that he had gained the prize he was after. A large animal was gripped in his talons.

Rick continued to watch, first with fascination, then with growing apprehension. Boss began to fly crazily and erratically, still gripping his prize. Finally, he wheeled abruptly, crashed headlong into a nearby cliff, and plummeted to the valley floor.

Rick was stunned by this strange turn of events and he determined to find out what had happened. He marked the place where he had last seen Boss fall and then laboriously began to climb down into the valley to see if he could find him. He searched over an hour before he came upon the stricken eagle with his dead prey still in his grip. The strange events were immediately explained. Boss's prize was a badger, one of the meanest and most ferocious animals alive. The scenario was obvious. Boss had gotten his prize, but the badger was no easy victim. He retaliated by gnawing away at the stomach of the eagle. Boss's prize was his undoing. Having claimed it, he couldn't let it go.

Listening to that moving tale, it occurred to me that sometimes we need deliverance not only from our defeats but from our victories. Clinging to our blessings, to God's mighty acts in the past, will undo us. We cannot coast on these indefinitely. We bring our praise and our prayers and say, "God help me." But when he does so, that very help may lead to new problems. The place of deliverance can become a place of persecution and death, as it was for the Israelites. Our deliverance rests on God alone, not on a particular place or circumstance.

What does this mean specifically? Let's say you are jobless and you pray and God answers your prayer. You get a job. What happens next? That very job can become the source of anxiety. You complain to your spouse or your friends, perhaps along these lines: "My job is killing me. My boss is unfair. My coworkers are undermining me. The new management doesn't appreciate all the years I have served." Your place of deliverance has become uninhabitable.

Let's say you are single and lonely and you pray about it. Eventually, God delivers you, and you marry. Your troubles just begin. God gave you a good gift, but that gift is somebody fallible who will fail you and disappoint you more than once—sometimes beyond the point of reconciliation. Marriage is a gift and a blessing, but it's not a safe place.

Or perhaps you want deliverance from poverty. Most of the world today is hungry and God must abhor that. You may be praying for just enough to pay the bills and take care of your family. But if those prayers are answered, it seems to me we have more fears and more anxieties. Henri Nouwen, a Harvard faculty member and a Roman Catholic priest and author, has lived in South America among the poorest of the poor. He said, "They were not fearful people. Where I found poverty, I found more joy and a sense of peace, less fear than among those who have so much." Nouwen stresses an important truth. Once we acquire things, we've got to protect them. Someone might take them away from us. Protection can range from a simple burglar system to, on a national scale, armies and nuclear weapons. With the blessing of wealth comes fear and anxiety.

Certainly it is legitimate to pray for deliverance from hunger. But for the most part, in our nation, God has answered those prayers. Our problem is that we are a nation of fatties. My doctor once said to me, "Larson, let me put it to you this way. You're an addict, and your grocer is a pusher." Having enough food is carried to excess. We are caught up in the esoteric eddies of Nouvelle Cuisine or sushi, granola or sunflower seeds. For the thirsty, there's always Perrier water.

God can deliver us from our inner problems as well, but even that deliverance is transitory. For example, we may pray about our lack of self-worth. We all need to have dignity. We aspire to be important. When those prayers are answered, we are in demand. In some cases, people all over the country or the world suddenly seem to need our smarts and our skills. *Time* magazine recently reported on the many famous people who have a phobia about planes and are nevertheless constantly flying. Among them are André Previn, Joanne Woodward, Bob Newhart, Jackie Gleason—even Ronald Reagan. In an interview done aboard *Air Force I*, the president was asked if he had overcome the fear of flying. "Overcome it!" he retorted, "I'm holding this plane up by sheer will power." Importance and power may lead to all sorts of scary new experiences from which we need to be delivered.

God is a delivering God. We see that not only in Exodus, but in our own lives. He wants us to have meaningful work, enough to eat, enough to live on. He wants to give us dignity and love. God has acted, and we can expect deliverance. But keep in mind that each new deliverance as a church, as a nation, as an individual, as a family, is a potential pitfall, and that's the way God intended it. He doesn't want us to wallow around in our personal Egypt. Our security is in Him.

I heard about a man who announced to his wife at breakfast that he was going to ask his employer for a raise. "I'm grossly underpaid," he said, "and I think today is the day to ask for a raise." He came home that night with good news. He got the raise. In the meantime, his wife had prepared a festive dinner—candles, flowers, cloth napkins—the works. Beside his plate was this note: "Darling, I knew you'd get the raise. I'm so proud of you. I hope this meal will tell you how much I love you."

Dinner over, he was helping to clear the table when he discovered a second note under his wife's plate. Here's what it said: "Darling, I know you're disappointed. You and I both know that you deserved that raise, but it doesn't matter. I love you, and I hope this special dinner will tell you that." The story makes a point I hope I'll remember for a long time. A raise is good; no raise is bearable. But life is more than raises or no raises.

Faith is an exodus, a perilous journey in which God delivers us over and over again. God provides us with food, water, camels, and resting places. But none of these things are intended to provide ultimate security and satisfaction. No oasis is permanent. It is not just deliverance we seek, but the Deliverer.

2. Help Is on the Way

If I were trying to find a title for the second chapter of Exodus, I think I'd call it "God Remembers." He remembered the Israelites, and He remembers us. He knows where we are. He knows about our particular pain, our hurts, our confusion, the shame and guilt in our lives. He cares. Help is on the way. Faith is simply trusting that God knows and that help is on the way before we see any evidence of it.

The main theme of this chapter stresses the problems of the Israelites, some of which we discussed in the last chapter. The new Pharaoh has begun all sorts of terrible, unfair measures to persecute them. This "problem theme" is all too familiar to those of us in this last half of the twentieth century. Injustice, hunger, crime, depravity of all kinds are rampant. We are threatened by nuclear war and a new deadly disease for which there is, as yet, no cure. Then there is our ever-present personal pain of illness, separation, and death. But this portion of Exodus features a minor theme, a sub-melody, if you will, and that is God's intervention, His aggressive love. He is at work for the Israelites and for us. He has not forgotten.

In the midst of this relentless persecution, a Hebrew woman of faith has a baby boy. What a woman! She is shrewd and wise and devises a scheme to save her child's life. She sets him adrift on a river to be found by the Egyptian princess. How carefully she must have planned it all! When and where did the princess come to bathe? How far and how fast would the current take the reed basket? When should her daughter, Miriam, appear, and what should she say? The poignancy of the story moves us. After wet-nursing the infant, she must give him up forever; and giving up our children, even at eighteen or twenty-one, is one of the hardest things we parents have to do.

Nevertheless, if we love them, we must at some point release them and back off from an active role in their affairs. In order to save Moses' life, his mother had to let him go, while he was still a toddler. We might wonder if she occasionally caught glimpses of him in the ensuing years—watched him turn from boy to teenager and reach manhood. Her role must have required remarkable discipline and sacrifice, and she must have wondered more than once where and if God was at work.

In retrospect, we see how exactly this was all part of God's plan. Moses could not have been the deliverer of his people had he not known the workings of the court of Pharaoh intimately. He had years to absorb the politics of the land and to become acquainted with those in power. His adoption by the Egyptian princess prepared him for the task God had for him. As a young man, his life took an unexpected new direction. In a rash moment, he killed the overseer oppressing the Hebrews.

I, for one, don't believe that murder, any murder, is part of God's plan. Moses took vengeance into his own hands, and vengeance is always God's prerogative, not ours. But even that circumstance served a purpose. The fear of discovery and punishment sent him into exile in the wilderness, where he married and fathered children and lived for the next forty years, a long interlude indeed, and surely one in which he must have felt forgotten by God.

But again, he was being prepared—prepared to take three million people into a barren wilderness for another forty years and train them to survive. During those forty years in Midian, Moses kept sheep. Friends who have been shepherds tell me that sheep are the most stubborn, mean, ornery animals around—not unlike the Israelites, not unlike you and me. Perhaps Moses learned to shepherd difficult people by herding uncooperative sheep, year after year.

In the midst of the blackest days of persecution in Egypt, help was on the way. God was preparing someone to deliver His people. Help was on the way for the Israelites, and it is for you and me, because God is a God who remembers. That help, in my experience, almost always comes in human form. God delivered the Israelites through Moses, a man prepared from childhood on to lead this unwieldy, often cantankerous throng into a new land. For those of us in the new covenant, deliverance is made possible through God's own Son, Jesus Christ, the risen Lord, King of Kings, Lord of Lords, and not through creeds and doctrines and a "right set of beliefs."

If you live in any good-sized city, you have surely been approached at least once by a panhandler, usually claiming to be hungry and asking for help. Suppose for a moment your reply went something like this: "You're hungry, friend? Listen, I just happen to have what you need here. It's a recipe for a fish stew. Just add a little salt pork and fish to some potatoes and onions and milk, and you'll have a marvelous supper. This is really a great recipe. Try it." The absurdity of that response is obvious. The hungry don't need recipes. Neither do the spiritually hungry. They don't need to hear philosophies and doctrines. Hungry people need someone to feed them. They need the bread of life and the living water in the person of Jesus Christ.

I would stake my life on the soundness and truth of every tenent in the Apostles' Creed, but the creed points to a person—Jesus, the Incarnate God. The Bible is, for Christians, the only infallible rule of faith and practice, but it is not the center of our faith. Jesus Himself said, "You diligently study the Scriptures, because you think that by them you possess eternal life. These are the Scriptures that testify about me, yet you refuse to come to me to have life" (John 5:39). Jesus is our deliverer and by His presence and power we are to be codeliverers. We are to let others know that help is on the way and to personally embody that help.

I had dinner recently with a young couple, both of whom are now involved in Christian ministry. The husband told a moving story about his background. He became addicted to drugs while still a teenager. By adulthood, he was hopelessly hooked. Life was one fix after another—nothing else mattered. At rock-bottom, he returned to his parents' home, desperate, destitute, devastated. He seemed to have nothing more to live for.

His mother, frantic over what was happening to her beloved son, was determined to find help for him. Late one night, she called the pastor of a nearby church—no one she knew, just a number from the yellow pages. The results were discouraging. The young pastor rarely made house calls and then only on parishioners in emergency situations. The call seemed pointless, but it wasn't.

Shortly after that phone conversation, the pastor went to bed but found himself unable to sleep. He could not seem to dismiss the anxious mother's call. After some prayer about the situation, he knew what he had to do. He got up, dressed, hopped in his car, and went to see the troubled young man. It was a life-changing night for my friend. It was the beginning of his faith and the end of his long enslavement to drugs.

As we sat over a beautifully appointed dinner table, these tales of a former life seemed remote and unreal. But my friend does not forget for a moment his dramatic rescue. While he was unable to help himself, God was preparing someone to intervene. Help was on the way in the form of a weary but obedient young pastor.

Sometimes we have a hard time believing that. We give in to doubts and discouragement. One of our sons was on the verge of marrying a young Jewish woman, a brilliant and wonderful girl whom we all loved. Since he was considering the ministry, we had many concerns about this alliance and did a lot of praying about it. The young woman, let's call her Ellen, had visited Seattle on several occasions, had heard the gospel presented strongly, clearly, and winsomely from all sorts of people, and yet seemed as far off as ever from the household of faith. It seemed her heart, like Pharaoh's, "was hardened."

In time, Ellen took a new job in Washington D.C., an important and influential job which brought her into contact with many well-known people. In the first few months, she spent time with both Billy Graham and Chuck Colson. One of her first new friends was a congressman's wife, a devout Christian and the owner of a Washington shop into which Ellen just happened to wander one afternoon. This new friend invited Ellen to meet her pastor, a Jewish Christian. In the space of the next few months, Ellen "just happened" to meet two other Jewish Christian pastors.

But further help was on the way. The congressman's wife invited her to a party and she was introduced to an interesting woman. The two were soon in deep conversation. Ellen learned that the other party guest and her pastor husband had visited Israel, in fact, had been missionaries to the Jews. In Ellen's words, "I gave up at that point." She was overwhelmed that God had gone to such lengths to make Himself known to her. She and the pastor's wife left the party and found a quiet place to pray together. Now Ellen is a Christian and more—she's witnessing, visiting prisons, and giving generously for God's causes.

In all those months, years, of desperate prayer, we family members had almost given up believing that help was on the way—and what help! In the course of a year, Ellen was inundated with people who loved her and loved the Lord. In her case, God seemed to field His best team in, of all places, the sophisticated and cynical city of Washington D.C.

The story of Moses' early years points up another important aspect of the life of faith. Nothing is wasted. We Christians believe in the sovereignty of God, that He is the ruler who uses everything in life to bring about His will. It's an especially important doctrine in Presbyterian theology, and yet, as a Presbyterian pastor, there were years when I had a hard time believing it. I was convinced that thirteen years of my life had been wasted.

I was working in a para-church ministry, one I believed in so strongly that it seemed to demand all my time, energy, even money. We had little of the latter in those years, but we poured all of the royalties from early books into this all-consuming mission. I traveled extensively, leaving my wife and three young children on their own almost every weekend. I believed I was renewing the church. It was all worth it.

And yet, at the end of those thirteen years, I left that work feeling wounded, unappreciated, betrayed by old friends and teammates. I felt the need for distance, and moved to an island off the Florida coast. I especially remember sitting on a seawall overlooking San Carlos Bay on the Fourth of July 1976, our nation's two hundredth birthday. I was all alone in the warm tropical night, watching rocket flares light up the distant sky and feeling they were somehow signaling the end of my productive ministry. Those thirteen years had all been for naught, or so it seemed.

God had no more use for me. The church was far from renewed, and I was burned out and disillusioned.

It was almost four years later that I was called to the pastorate in Seattle. God had healed me by then, and I could see at last that nothing had been wasted. Those Florida years were incredibly creative. I had completed a research project, written two books and coauthored three more. I began to realize that those thirteen years of para-church ministry had prepared me for reentering the pastorate in a unique way. God had given me the opportunity to study the church in America from coast to coast, its glories and foibles. I had had grassroots training in small groups, lay-witness, fund raising, administration. But, even more significant: had I not left that work, however unhappily, I would not be where I am now, and I want to tell you that these are the best and most rewarding years of my life.

We find that Moses was prepared all along the way for his role; but, first of all, by his mother. Did that shrewd, faith-filled woman have any idea what was ahead for her beloved little son? Mothers are often instrumental in shaping their children's destiny. Don Morgan, a friend of mine in Connecticut, lost his mother when he was a small boy. A year or so ago, he learned about a strange incident that occurred just before her death.

She was talking about the family she was soon to be leaving and trying to make some provision for their future welfare. "Are you worried about Donny?" a friend asked. "He's going to be all right," was the reply. "He is going to serve God all the days of his life."

Thirty-four years later, her son, now a pastor, heard this prophecy, and it gave him a special bond with his long-dead mother. "How could she have known?" he marvels. His life was changed by the faith of a mother he never knew, who believed for him. He and Moses have that in common.

Apart from Pharaoh's vendetta against Hebrew male infants, Moses would not have been prepared to be the deliverer. Certainly that wicked scheme was not part of God's plan. But, again, those circumstances were used for good. The Israelites found that their enemies could be used by God. That's still true. God can use even those people who do not wish you well, to put you where He wants you, and to bless you. We all know what it means to be paranoid. It is to believe everybody hates you. But if you think everybody loves you, believe me, that's a disease too. Everybody doesn't love you. But in God's master plan for you, it doesn't matter. He will use your friends and enemies alike to bring about His will.

Pharaoh, the child-murderer, is ultimately part of God's plan for deliverance. The murder Moses committed was used for good in God's plan, though hatred and murder are never His will. We're reminded again that there are no heroes in the Bible. There are just weak and faithless people, like ourselves. Moses committed a crime. Nevertheless, he was, through it all, being prepared to be the deliverer. God remembers. We need to believe that even as we pray.

And speaking of prayer, we need to make those prayers positive. Too often our prayers are born of desperation—"Lord, I have no job." "Lord, I am sick." "Lord, my child's in trouble." "Lord, I'm afraid." Those prayers of desperation are some kind of mechanical incantation to keep the bad things from happening. Why not try instead to picture the answers even as you pray. Jesus said, "Whatever you ask for in prayer, believe that you have received it, and it will be yours" (Mark 11:24). As an act of faith, believe that help is on the way and picture the form that help will take. Your mind can be an instrument for bringing about God's will.

Late in his long and eventful career, Winston Churchill, the great British statesman, was asked to address the graduating class at Cambridge. With slow and deliberate steps, he mounted the lectern, hung his cane on the podium, and surveyed his audience for several minutes in silence. The first three words, delivered in his unforgettable tones, were, "Never give up," He paused and repeated himself. "Never give up." With one final glance at his audience, he added a closing sentence: "Never give up," and, just as deliberately, took his seat. The auditorium erupted in wild applause.

It's a message we would all do well to remember whenever we feel God has abandoned us. Over the Christmas holidays I conducted a funeral for a nineteen year old. The young man had taken his life in despair over an unhappy love affair. I didn't know him personally and so had no way of knowing whether this last desperate act was at all predictable somewhere along the way. It must have seemed in that final hour that there was neither hope nor help. That tragedy pointed up anew for me the obligation you and I have to let those hurting and hopeless people around us know that help is on the way. Martin Luther claimed that faith is saying, "nevertheless . . ." However bad our present situation, nevertheless God cares. God remembers. Never give up.

3. When God Speaks

An old friend from Alabama tells of going to a Christian conference many years ago. He had never been to anything of the kind before, and the first meeting he attended was especially discouraging.

He was in a group of about twelve people, and they had been asked by the leader to share what God had been saying to them recently. The reports from those around the circle were impressive. "God told me to go on a diet" . . . "I feel God speaking to me about the way I use my time" . . . "I think God is asking me to forgive my mother" . . . They had all reported except my friend, Coleman, and he found all eyes fastened on him expectantly. In the thickest Alabama accent you've ever heard, he blurted, "Ahm sorry . . . but de Lawd ain't nevah opened His mouf to me."

In subsequent years, Coleman loved telling that story on himself because from that weekend on, he began a new level of communication with "de Lawd." But it seems to me, Christians are often divided into those who have never heard God speak and those who always seem to be hearing God speak. There is a lot of confusion on this issue.

Three chapters into the book of Exodus, we find God speaking to Moses and—assuming He is the same God yesterday, today, and forever—this account of His encounter with Moses must be consistent with the way He continues to work to direct your life and mine. Nevertheless, we are more often than not baffled about exactly how this takes place. If God is able to speak to us, then we need to address some of the questions that raises—more specifically, where does He speak? When does He speak? How does He speak? And what does He say?

Moses first heard God speak as he tended sheep in the desert, something he had been doing, as we said, for forty years. It must have seemed a day much like any other day when God suddenly and dramatically caught his attention by means of a burning bush. Actually, such a sight is not all that uncommon in hot, dry, desert country. Thornbushes, full of resin and sap, occasionally burst into flame. The phenomenon is the result of spontaneous combustion. But this particular bush was not extinguished in a moment. It continued to burn and was not consumed. Intrigued, Moses "turned aside to see this great sight."

Biblically, fire has always been a sign of God's presence—a fire that burns but does not consume. The fire of God accompanied the coming of the Holy Spirit at Pentecost. On that occasion, as recounted in the second chapter of Acts, a wind filled the Upper Room and there were tongues as of fire. Those present experienced the fulfillment of God's promise that He would send His Spirit to live in everyone who received Him.

Even in more recent history, fire continues to be linked with God's presence. Blaise Pascal was a famous Christian mystic, in addition to being a scientific wizard. While still a young man, he invented the adding machine, the barometer, the first bus system in Paris. Upon his death, a paper was found in the lining of the coat he habitually wore. It proved to be a written account of his conversion experience. "From about half past ten in the evening until about half past twelve," he wrote, "fire." Pascal kept the record of that mysterious life-changing night close at hand the remainder of his life.

Dwight Moody, one of the great evangelists of this century, tells of a similar event. For a long time he prayed along these lines: "Lord, I want to contain all of you that I can. Give me all of you that I can hold." One day he was walking down the street of a great city when he felt a sudden burning in his heart. It increased in intensity to the extent that he was forced to find a hotel room and lie down. Still the burning continued. Moody began to pray that it would cease. He felt he couldn't bear any more. But from that point on, God's fire consumed Moody, and he became a blazing force for the Kingdom all over the world.

As we said, it was through fire, a flaming bush that was not consumed, that Moses had his attention arrested. But from that bush, God called Moses by name. He left no doubt about who was the cause of this strange sight, or for whose benefit it occurred. He wanted a personal encounter. I was told about a little five-year-old boy who was lost in a huge department store. In desperation, he called out his mother's name—"Marjorie, Marjorie!" In seconds she came running, greatly relieved to find him. "Oh, honey," she said, "I'm so glad to see you. Why didn't you call 'Mommy' instead of 'Marjorie'?" "I tried that," he explained. "You'd be surprised how many wrong mommies came."

God could have called out, "Sinner, Sinner!" There are a lot of us around. He was talking to a particular sinner. He was talking to Moses. God not only calls us by name, He usually has a specific message for us. He did with Abraham. He asked him to leave Ur of the Chaldees and start a journey to a new land. He spoke to Samuel, the small boy who was sent off by his mother to serve the priest, Eli, in the temple. The lad was awakened by a voice calling his name. Puzzled, he hurried off to ask Eli if he had called. "No, go back to bed," was the response. This scenario was repeated three times, until it dawned on Samuel that God was speaking to him, and giving him a task.

Isaiah was sitting in worship when God's living presence filled the temple and called him. Mary was drawing water when God spoke to her through an angel and asked her to undertake the most important task in history. In the ninth chapter of Acts, God spoke to Paul while he was traveling. He had set out to arrest and punish Christians, which he thought was God's will. In the middle of that journey, God called out, "Saul, Saul, why are you persecuting *me?*" In Damascus, Ananias heard God's call to visit Saul and pray with him.

You and I know dozens and perhaps hundreds of Christians who have been stopped in their tracks by some unusual event which caught their attention for the first time. But there is a problem. How do we know whether it is actually God speaking? I'm sure Moses had some doubts. Certainly, Ananias must have had misgivings when he was told to go to talk to this man named Saul. Ananias must have been well aware of who Saul of Tarsus was and how dangerous this task might prove to be. It would be like telling a Jew in Nazi Germany, "Go to Joseph Mengele in that brutal concentration camp and tell him that God loves him." But faith requires that we act in spite of our misgivings. We must walk in the light we've been given before we can expect more light.

In terms of guidance, only one thing seems certain. God's will is that we not always know His will. Unfortunately, many of us have been misled on that score. We assume that once we become Christians, filled with the Spirit, every move we make will be guided. This is not so. We don't doubt that sometimes God speaks clearly, but He does not always do so. The book of Acts is full of the mistakes of the early church. Guidance was not infallible. The first post-resurrection apostle, chosen by lot, was Matthias, who is never heard from or about again. Surely the apostle Paul was already God's choice for the twelfth apostle. Later on, Paul and Barnabas could not agree on whether or not John Mark should come along on their second missionary journey. The controversy caused them to go their separate ways.

We conclude that even the disciples were not always in agreement over God's will. God wants to have a relationship with us, and we wouldn't need Him if we always knew His will. The Bible, prayer, Christian friends—all these are important avenues for finding God's will. Yet, sometimes we act entirely in blind faith uncertain of the outcome.

When and where does God speak? In the Bible, God so often speaks in the ordinary routine of daily life. We think we must hear Him as the result of some hallucinatory experience, or in some holy place—a convent, a sanctuary, on a mountaintop, or during some quiet retreat. But God spoke to Moses while he was doing what he did every day—keeping sheep. As we said, Isaiah had his great vision of God while worshiping. Paul was traveling and Mary was drawing water. The disciples were mending their nets and taking care of their every-day fishing chores when Jesus called them, "Follow me."

Our oldest son, Peter, was thirty-two years old when he heard God speak to him. He is presently in seminary, heading for the ministry, and the only person more surprised than I is Peter. Where did God speak? In a jeep between Dallas and Tyler, Texas. Peter picked up a young hitchhiker who, as it turned out, had just been released from prison. His passenger began to talk about Jesus Christ and an earlier experience as a believer. According to Peter, they both had an uncanny sense of God's presence. The jeep seemed to be filled with the fire and light of His Spirit.

Back in Tyler, and still in the glow of this mystical experience, Peter sought out his best friend, a down-to-earth lawyer and businessman, and related the amazing story to him. A year and a half later, when our son was questioning God's call and debating whether or not to go to seminary, he discussed his dilemma with this same friend, Ted.

"Peter," said Ted, "I don't know much about God. I only know how you looked after that experience in your jeep. You looked like the little girl Stephen King described in his novel *Firestarter*, whose hair sometimes seemed to be on fire. Ever since you shared that story with me, I've been praying to the God you met in your jeep. That was surely God, and you'd better be true to that experience." Where does God speak? Sometimes in a jeep on a Texas highway.

When God speaks, it sometimes complicates our lives. It's like falling in love. A young friend recently showed me a love letter she had received. It read, "Oh my darling, since I met you I can't eat or sleep. I'm in torment, every minute of every hour, wondering if you love someone else. I dread the possibility that I might lose you. I'm in agony, fearing that you don't really love me. Every second I'm afraid you'll decide I'm not good enough for you, and heartsick because I know I'm not. Oh, my darling, I'm more miserable than I've ever been in my life. It's the best thing that ever happened to me." A contradiction? Not necessarily. Having fallen in love with God, I don't always feel good, and the path ahead is often fraught with danger and difficulties, but it is still the best thing that ever happened to me.

Those places where God speaks are forever holy in your life and mine. There are those specific places where I know God dealt with me, just as He did with Moses in the burning bush. I shared one of those holy moments in Stuttgart, Germany, in the first chapter. About ten years ago, I felt prompted to go back and find that building. It had been demolished in the intervening years and new structures now stand on that site. But my memory of that holy place is vivid and lasting.

I once heard God speak in a field near Minocqua, Wisconsin. I was with my long-time friend, Lloyd Ogilvie, and we were at the time just out of seminary and starting our ministries. We built a pile of rocks, like those Ebenezer described so often in the Old Testament, and made a covenant with the Lord. Our prayers went something like this: "Lord, we want to be your people. We pray you will use us to build your church." I'm sure I could never find that place today. But in my mind, those stones are still remembered and that covenant is genuine. Lloyd and I can only go back in memory to that holy place where God did business with us.

Years later God spoke to me one afternoon in the middle of the Gulf of Mexico, on an occasion when I very nearly drowned. I was shelling on a desert island when a storm came up and swept my small boat into the surf. I plunged in and started swimming after it and, before I knew it, the tide had carried me far beyond the point of return. I was exhausted and ready to give up when God seemed to say, "Stop struggling and tread water." The verse that came, oddly enough, was from Exodus, "Stand still and see the salvation of God." I was still treading water three hours later when a tugboat appeared out of nowhere and rescued me. That particular body of water on the Florida coast will always be a holy place for me.

When God speaks, He initiates a dialogue and a response is required. It is a mysterious dialogue, sometimes hard to explain or rationalize. There is a woman in our congregation named Mrs. Chan. She is a tiny woman, energetic and faith-filled. Last year she came to a member of the staff with a pressing problem. Her daughter and son-in-law were on the verge of divorce. The problem, according to Mrs. Chan, was that her son-in-law was not a Christian. If he could just be converted, all would be well.

She had been praying about all this for some time and felt she had clear guidance. She planned to send the young man plane fare to Seattle. She would bring him to church, and he would give his life to Jesus. She was hoping he could be baptized that very afternoon. Could that be arranged? The pastor she spoke with tried to dissuade her, to help her see the foolishness of this plan. He found himself saying things like: "God doesn't operate that way, Mrs. Chan. You can't manipulate Him or your son-in-law like that. His being in church one Sunday isn't likely to produce the kind of results you want."

When this interview was shared with the staff, we all concurred that our colleague had handled it wisely. We didn't know, until much later, that his advice had gone unheeded. Mrs. Chan sent the plane fare and the young man worshiped with us. It just happened to be one of the few Sundays a year when I felt prompted to make an invitation after the sermon to those who wanted to start the life of faith for the first time. She was waiting in the narthex after the service—her son-in-law in tow. "He came, Reverend Larson," she said, beaming, "and when you gave the invitation, he gave his life to God." Sure enough, the new convert was grinning and nodding his head.

Unlike our less-than-faith-filled staff, Mrs. Chan was not at all surprised. God spoke, she acted, and her daughter's husband came into the Kingdom. I don't believe God always works this way, but we need to be reminded that He does sometimes. Faith is not an exact science.

God revealed His plans to Mrs. Chan just as He did to Moses. But when Moses was to carry out those plans, he protested. "Not me. I can't do that. I stutter." When God continued to insist, Moses said, "Who shall I tell them has sent me?" In response, God said two pivotal things. First of all, He said, "Tell them I am the God of Abraham, of Isaac and of Jacob." The Hebrew people needed to know that the God who spoke to Moses was the same God they worshiped—the God of their fathers and their grandfathers and their great-grandfathers and all the rest of their antecedants.

Further, Moses was to say that "I Am" has sent him. "I Am Who I Am." The person of God is a mystery. Nobody knows His will perfectly, but we watch and trust and wait to see what He will do with us and with the world. The dialogue, once begun, is open-ended. We give God our lives, and as we begin to abide more and more in Him, He reveals more of His plan. In Moses' case, the dialogue began at the burning bush, but it continued for the next forty years.

We started this chapter with some questions, and I think the answers can be found not only in the biblical record but within the framework of your experience and mine.

Does God speak? Yes. Emphatically, yes.

Where does He speak? Anywhere and everywhere, but those are forever after holy places.

When does He speak? Whenever we are listening.

How does He speak? Through the Bible, through Christian friends, through circumstances, through prayer.

As for what He says, that's open-ended. But, in all the cases we have examined, it is a personal message, just for you, and it usually concerns the direction of your life. The dialogue with Moses changed history. The dialogue He has with you might do the same.

4. Anyone But Me

Most of the time I love the pastorate. So much of what I do is satisfying. I enjoy preaching, teaching, counseling, ministering to those who are ill or in trouble. I even enjoy overseeing our large and diverse staff and hammering out new directions with our governing body, the Session.

But now that we as a church find ourselves in the middle of a much-needed building program, many less-pleasant tasks have taken up a good deal of my time. For the most part, I do not like calling on faithful parishioners, suggesting they might like to give generously to the building fund. I do not like slugging it out with the various community representatives and city agencies, who are unconvinced of the rightness of this step. I do not like being caught in the middle of the different factions within the church family who are pressing to get things done their way. In the past year I have been feeling anxious and oppressed more often than I like to admit, and many nights have passed with a minimum of sleep. I find myself wishing I could escape into a more spiritual role with extended quiet time to read the Word and nourish my own soul, to feed the birds and bless little children. Moses' quiet life in the Midian desert looks awfully attractive.

Perhaps that is why I have a new appreciation for his initial response to God's call to begin negotiating with Pharaoh for the release of the Israelites. I think he grasped immediately what a radical life change this new task would entail. He says, "Lord, anyone but me. Don't you have someone else you can send?" I think his response can be attributed as much to stage fright as to humility. He also appears to have serious questions about God's strategy. Is it possible that God is misinformed about the unlimited powers of Pharaoh, or the intractable mind-set of the elders of Israel? If He really understood the situation, He wouldn't expect to get this task accomplished easily.

Moses was being asked to bring about reform from the top down. That's much different from instigating a grassroots revolution, the sort of thing the apostle Paul did so much of in his missionary journeys. In the beginning of his ministry, that's how he undertook the spreading of the gospel. He gathered little groups of believers into worshiping communities all over Asia Minor and eventually throughout Europe. But before long, Paul was also required to stand before kings and governors, the power structure of his time, and give his witness. I think most of us are more comfortable working at the grassroots level, but sometimes God requires us to confront those at the top—of the company, the city, perhaps even the nation—with His message.

As Christians, you and I are called to be liberators. When God got your attention at some burning bush, He commissioned you to make a difference somewhere, some place. Where and how we do that is, of course, unique. Suppose you were asked to go to the president with some particular demand—like a halt to nuclear arms. In any cross-section of churchgoers, I'd say 90 percent would feel inadequate in such a situation. We tend to say, "I'm not good enough to do that. I don't have the ego strength or the verbal skills."

Our feelings of inadequacy are really a form of sin. We have all sorts of excuses why we can't undertake some important work for God. Certainly, Moses could have asked to be excused, simply on the grounds of his age. He was, in human terms, too old to embark on a radical career change. Most of us tend to retreat from risky living on the basis of being too young or too old. We have infirmities, physical or emotional, real or imagined. We have too many responsibilities, or too little education. These excuses are rooted more in fear of failure than in humility.

We have only to look around to realize the diversity of people God is using—the formerly addicted, the disadvantaged, the handicapped, the very young, and the very old. I recently read about an eighty-seven-year-old lady named Huldah Crooks who began mountain climbing at sixty-six. She has climbed the highest mountain in North America—Mount Whitney—twenty-one times. "At thirty-three," she says, "I prayed for the rest that would come with death. I was so tired." At sixty-six she apparently got her second wind, and she's been on the go—upward—ever since.

One woman in our congregation has an unusual story. Her husband is retired, and I would surmise she is well past middle-age, though those things are hard to guess. She had been feeling for some time that God had given her a special ministry to those who are hospitalized. She loved calling on patients and trying to impart something of God's love through scripture messages, through prayer, through friendship and concern.

She began to sense God wanted her to do this on some continuing basis in one of our local hospitals. This is a woman, mind you, with no special training in counseling or pastoral calling. Nevertheless, she presented herself to the administrator of one of our local hospitals one morning and declared that she would very much like to come on staff as their chaplain—unpaid, of course. To her amazement, he responded positively, "That's just what we've needed here. I've been hoping we could find our way to make a chaplain available in an unofficial kind of role. You're on."

That all happened over ten years ago. My friend now spends several days a week doing what she loves most, ministering to the sick. This far-from-ordinary, untrained layperson is the hospital chaplain, the only one they've got, and an unofficial but integral part of all staff meetings. She could so easily have felt her dreams were unrealistic. But hers was not an "anyone but me" attitude. If a chaplain was needed, she had a clear directive. "Why not me?"

Nevertheless, Moses was reluctant, and many of us can identify with that. He needed reassurance, and God supplied it. When he continued to insist the people would not listen to him,

God asked a strange question. "What's in your hand?" Moses was carrying a rod, a shepherd's crook. God proceeded to show him how that ordinary symbol of office could become an extraordinary instrument of divine power—one he could make use of in the encounter with Pharaoh.

That question, "What's in your hand?" is still relevant, as you and I contemplate undertaking some task we feel God has given us. It may be your youth or your maturity. It could be your job, or even your joblessness. You may have something positive, like energy, talent, and creativity. You may be holding on to something negative, like destructive habits or self-pity. Whatever is in your hand, plus or minus, God can and will use it.

One of the great presidents of what is today Princeton University was Jonathan Edwards. This great revival preacher came to that post with only failure in his hands. He had been fired from the Massachusetts church he was serving. In disgrace and jobless, he happened to be available to head up one of our great educational institutions.

Next, God reassured Moses about his lack of eloquence. "I will help you speak and will teach you what to say" (Exodus 4:12). He had only to go to Pharaoh and open his mouth and God would put words into it. It's a promise similar to the one Jesus made to His disciples; and we see, over and over again, how that promise was kept, as we read the accounts of their many appearances before tribunals and councils. These ordinary, uneducated men confounded the wise and the powerful.

God's promise to supply the right words at the right time is one we can still rely on. Years ago during a prolonged steel strike in Pittsburgh, a layman named Dave Griffith felt God was trying to bring about reconciliation. He felt directed to try to call on both the union heads and the steel company executives and ask, "What is it God would want you to do?" Now, Dave had a serious, almost crippling, stutter. Nevertheless, he went and, strangely enough, before long the strike was settled. Much later, one of the executives told me why the warring factions had listened to Dave in the first place. "Nobody with a stutter like that would wade into that ticklish situation on his own power. God had to be in it."

Moses' next move was to get confirmation of this call of God from his family. He first discussed the matter with Jethro, his father-in-law, in whose household he had been living for the last four decades. Would Jethro give him permission to return to Egypt and find his kinsman? Surprisingly, the answer was, "Go in peace." Let's try to keep that in mind the next time we are tempted to hide from God's call behind our duty to our family. We say, "I can't do that. I've got kids in college. I've got a mortgage to pay. My wife . . . my in-laws . . . my parents . . . need me."

I've been a member of a small group where people voicing those objections were challenged to ask the family how they felt about some particular new direction. I especially remember a New York friend who had an opportunity to teach in a small Episcopal, private school in Connecticut, the kind of job he had always wistfully longed for. He was nearly fifty years old and at the top of his profession. He was sure the move wouldn't be fair to his family. "I've got kids going to school. We've got a standard of living we're all used to." He was urged to go and ask them, and their response was overwhelmingly positive. "Dad, you do whatever you think God wants you to do." He had no hiding place. He gave up his highly paid job and went to teach at a modest salary, and the next years were the most fulfilling of his life.

With Jethro's blessing, then, "Moses took his wife and his sons and set them on an ass" and started off for Egypt. That was surely the hardest part—the first step of the adventure. It is for most of us. But once you start, God can guide you, even if you are going in the wrong direction. It's been said you can't steer a bicycle standing still. God can't steer us until we get going. Further guidance comes as we start.

From that point on, Moses was determined to follow God's orders and do it God's way. Killing the Egyptian had been

Moses' way. In the future, he was willing to have God call the shots in his dealings with the Egyptians. Moses started off with all the best intentions but, at a lodging place, a mysterious illness struck him, threatening his very life. His Arab wife, Zipporah, sensing divine displeasure in this turn of events, quickly performed circumcision on her young son. Next she touched Moses' feet with the foreskin, saying, "Surely you are a bridegroom of blood to me."

Can this strange story have any relevance for you and me? I think so. God seemed to indicate clearly that there was some unfinished business to take care of, in this case the circumcision, before they could continue on His mission. As God gives you and me a commission, there may be some things He has clearly told us to do that we have not yet done. Take care of that unfinished business. It may mean a public confession of faith and church membership. It may mean consistent and regular Bible study and prayer. We may need to be more responsible in the area of stewardship. As we take that next step, we can continue on our way with God's blessings.

Upon their arrival in Egypt, Moses and Aaron brought together all of the elders of the Israelites and received their blessing. That, it seems to me, was the final sign that this commission from God was genuine. It's the kind of blessing the apostle Paul sought in each new city during his many travels. He always preached first of all in the synagogue. Only if and when he was rejected there did he move on to preach and to teach outside of the existing religious structures. It's a strategy we need to keep in mind as we find the Body of Christ becoming more and more fragmented, with the passing of time and the conflicting claims of orthodoxy or heresy. I am moved by the efforts of Moses and Aaron to explain to and include those Hebrew elders and enlist their support.

God's pointed question to Moses at the burning bush is one he continues to ask: "What's in your hand?" It's a question that helps us sort out our own credentials for being codeliverers, those who can make a difference. They vary from person to person, of course, and you may think you have few. But it occurred to me that all of us have at least three positive attributes. First of all, we have time. Some younger people may have less time than they think they have. Some older people may have more time than they anticipate. But we all have a certain amount of time ahead of us, a little or a lot. Give God that time. It's your most precious commodity.

We all have money, though again, that may be very little or a whole lot. We can be stewards of whatever we have now and what we will have in the future. After all, money is a function of time—it is compensation for the sacrifice of time. It is given in exchange for a chunk of your life and your creative abilities.

Thirdly, we all have reputation and influence. There are people who know and trust you, however large or small that group may be. You may feel called to speak or act in a way that makes you look ridiculous before them. Will you do that? Moses risked that. That's what faith is all about.

An article in *Forbes* magazine a few years ago gave readers some unusual advice. "If you want happiness, take tranquilizers or pray for senility. Anxiety is inevitable and prolonged depression is normal." During the years on the Midian desert, Moses had a tranquil life. He was happily married, the father of healthy children, keeping sheep and living a good, clean, outdoor life. When God called, all that tranquility was over. Life became complicated, but the adventure began. After forty years of preparation, Moses' life took off.

God's call to you and me is meant to be disturbing, a call full of high risks and high adventure. We respond, beginning with what is in our hand—our time, our money, and our influence. God will use it all.

5. The Impossible Mission

Moses was given an impossible mission. His assignment was to invade the secular world of power and politics with specific and non-negotiable demands. It would be like being given the task of confronting the Russian leaders and demanding that they let all the people of Eastern Europe go. "Release them from the Communist Bloc. Let Germany be integrated. Remove the Berlin Wall. Free the people of Poland and Czechoslovakia." We can all appreciate the impossibility of that job.

Or, to use another parallel, suppose you felt God was requiring you to demand that the Irish Republican Army stop its terrorist acts against the people of Northern Ireland; or to insist that all the Protestants leave their homeland and go back to England, whence they came 350 years earlier. Using those present-day terms, we can begin to appreciate the radical nature of Moses' assignment.

We can only imagine how inadequate Moses felt about that assignment. God's business, as we have said, is always deliverance, and therefore it is our business. In the old covenant, believers followed the visions of a few chosen leaders, a patriarch, a prophet, a king. But in the new covenant, you and I are called to individual leadership. We have access to the Holy Spirit of God and we are to be deliverers someplace, some time, somehow. That is our task, and in that task Moses is our role model.

Moses, first of all, was obedient. In spite of his conviction that God had the wrong man, he agreed to go. His first efforts were an abysmal failure. Pharaoh was incensed that he and Aaron presumed to tell him what to do. His response was, "I don't know your God, and I will not let Israel go." But, from the beginning, Moses is simply overwhelmed by the seeming impossibility of his mission, as you and I often are if we really understand God's assignment for us.

Almost all worthwhile missions seem impossible at first. For the most part, they haven't been attempted before simply because they were so difficult. Our own Revolutionary War seemed a hopeless cause at the time. The tiny band of colonies, far from a cohesive political group or even of one mind, took on the might of the British Empire. One-third of the population was pro-British, and another third was neutral. Only a minority was committed to this costly and seemingly hopeless war. Imagine what it might have been like to have been a soldier at Valley Forge that fateful winter. Those troops, hungry and cold and with no proper equipment, must have considered theirs to be an impossible mission.

God is still giving His people tasks that, in the world's terms, seem doomed to failure. A country lawyer in Americus, Georgia, heard the word of the Lord about twenty years ago. Millard Fuller felt God was asking him to do something about the one billion people in the world who have inadequate housing, or no housing at all. I knew Millard in the days when he got that vision, and I tended to write him off as an impractical dreamer. Subsequently, the organization called Habitat for Humanity was born, and tens of thousands of homes have already been built or improved by means of interest-free loans and volunteer labor. Thanks to God's caring people, this impossible mission is becoming more and more possible.

A lay couple in our Seattle parish found themselves committed to a task that looked insurmountable. They were on an around-the-world junket when they contacted some missionaries to the Masai tribe in Kenya. The plight of these once-proud warriors moved Denny and Jeanne Grindall. This tribe is just one generation from extinction because of drought and reapportionment of land. Their cattle are no longer free to graze as they once were. Survival depends upon finding new food resources and stable water supplies. Denny and Jeanne, with no training, left their home in Seattle for six months every year to live in the arid Rift Valley. For the next thirteen years, they brought water, housing, schools, and churches to these stone-age people.

I often excuse my lack of faith, my reluctance to tackle difficult tasks, on the grounds that I am simply "being realistic." The Old Testament is sprinkled with stories of people of faith who acted in ways that seem, on the surface, far from sensible. We can imagine Noah's neighbors trying to convince him to be realistic. "Listen, Noah, this project is going to cost an enormous amount of money. Why would you build this huge boat miles from any water? It will take years to finish it. Your neighbors are at their wits' end, with all this hammering and sawing. Come on, Noah, be realistic."

Joshua, Moses' successor, was a general with some strange battle plans. I'm sure his advisors were urging him to be realistic. We can hear their advice. "Listen, General Joshua, this is an armed city—one of the strongholds of the world, with walls fourteen feet thick. We are a rag-tag bunch of desert wanderers. How can we attack a city by simply blowing horns? Be realistic." The realists, fortunately, did not prevail, and Jericho fell to the Israelites.

Gideon took on an army of thousands of heavily armed men with a force of three hundred. His secret weapons were clay jars, candles, and trumpets. I'm sure he had his detractors, pleading with him to "be realistic." David, wearing only a loincloth and carrying a simple slingshot, defeated an awesome giant who had terrorized the entire Israelite army. At least a few people in the crowd must have suggested that this young lad be realistic.

But there are a few incidents in both Old and New Testaments where faith gives way to this more realistic attitude we've been talking about. Abraham and Sarah, promised a child in their old age, literally laughed at God. When Peter was in prison, the faithful saints held a prayer meeting at the home of John Mark's mother, asking for his deliverance. Their prayers were interrupted by a knock on the door. The servant, Rhoda, answered it to find Peter standing on the threshold. When she announced his arrival, she was not believed. Those gathered disciples were too realistic to assume that their prayers could be answered so concretely and so immediately.

The first disciples had an impossible mission. They were not rabbis. They had no theological training. They were ordinary laymen, some civil servants and some businessmen. These men were commissioned to go into all the world and tell the good news. They did it, and we are here because they did it. They refused to be realistic.

A growing number of men and women in our parish have accomplished an impossible mission over the past few years. They have kicked addictions to alcohol, drugs, even food. But, in a sense, we all have addictions. That's part of our human frame. We may not be on booze or pills, but there are other addictions just as insidious—sex, overwork, negative thinking, fault-finding, shyness, self-pity, to name a few.

A good many people are addicted to worry. According to a recent magazine article, 40% of our time is spent worrying about things that never happen. 30% is spent fretting about things that can't be changed by all the worry in the world, old decisions that can't be reversed, for instance. 12% of worry time is over misinterpreting the feelings of others (i.e., why did she say that? what did he mean when he said that?). 10% is over our health, which only gets worse when we worry. That leaves about 8% for legitimate concern.

If you're a worrier, you know how helpless you feel when you try to overcome those anxieties which are so unproductive, which erode your confidence and trouble your sleep. We tackle that kind of impossible mission only by the power of God. But one way to tap into that power is to share those worries with someone in your support system—and I hope you have one. As one young child confided to her mother, "It's too much work to worry alone."

It's alarming to read that Moses obeyed God and things got worse—at least at the outset. Did that ever happen to you? He went to Pharaoh and his demand was refused. Pharaoh had no intention of letting those valuable slaves, perhaps by now three million in number, go. Furthermore, instead of resting from their burdens, these slaves were to make as many bricks as ever, except that no straw would be provided. The interview with Pharaoh resulted in increased oppression for the Israelites.

That's the way it seems sometimes for us. I heard about a nine-year-old whose sister who was just starting school. He gave her some advice. "Don't ever learn to spell 'cat,'" he warned. "Once you do that, they just keep on giving you harder words." Sometimes when you are on God's impossible mission, things only get harder. My advice is, "Enjoy it." Just say to yourself, "This is one of those days when I'm supposed to make bricks without straw." It's entirely biblical.

In 1519, that avaricious explorer, Hernando Cortez, landed in what is now Vera Cruz, Mexico, and established the first colony for Spain. As he took on the task of gaining gold for his sovereign, he announced they would be marching inland to conquer Montezuma, the local ruler. Lest there be any misunderstanding, he issued this order: "Burn the boats." So the ships that had carried them across the sea were destroyed. It is a drastic but courageous way to begin any journey of faith. Moses must have felt he had embarked on a course from which there was no way back, but he was still not entirely convinced of the rightness of it all.

In the fifth chapter of Exodus, he complains one more time about his assignment, and the gist of that complaint is, "God, why have you allowed all this? Why did you send me to Pharaoh in the first place?" God simply repeats His instructions and His promises, the most amazing of which is, "See, I make you as God to Pharaoh." In spite of his weaknesses, Moses is to have the power of God in his dealings with Pharaoh. The treasure of God's Spirit is always in earthen vessels, and if we set about the impossible mission, we are at times going to look like God to the people we are sent to. Our energy and love and creativity will astound even ourselves.

In Florida, where I used to live, the Mississuki Indians inhabit the Everglades. They are, among other things, great alligator wrestlers. One day, a tourist was talking to one of these Indians and commented on the necklace he was wearing. She wanted to know what it was made of. "Alligator teeth," was the reply. "Ah," continued the woman, "is that kind of like wearing a necklace of pearls?" "Not quite," he said. "Anybody can open an oyster." Our impossible mission may prove to be more like wrestling alligators than opening oysters, but God has promised us His resources, as He did Moses.

St. Francis, when he was called by the Lord, was given a commission: "Sell all that you have and give to the poor." This wealthy nobleman renounced his rights and sold all of his possessions, except for the clothes on his back. Then God gave him a second commission: "Rebuild my church." His response was to begin rebuilding a broken-down chapel in his town in Italy. He had to go out and beg money for the stones, boards, and mortar. Unable to afford a wheelbarrow, he was forced to carry all the materials on his back. Months later, with the old chapel finally rebuilt, he realized God had actually given him a much larger task. "Rebuild my church in the world." He set about to do that, and the rest is history. This intrepid man of God started a ministry that affected the whole Roman church and the entire Western world.

The task of rebuilding the church is an impossible mission in every age. The great question right now among Asian Christians is, "Can the West be converted?" Is it possible for those of us in America and Europe to go back to our Christian roots and use our wealth and resources to build God's kingdom and bring health and hope to the rest of the world? We could say that is the mission on which we all need to embark—to rebuild the church and to make it the glorious body of Christ it was meant to be.

One of our sons crossed the Sahara Desert a few years back and made an interesting discovery. He claims you could divide all the travelers making that journey into two different groups. There were the people who were intent on getting across the desert at any cost. Then there were those whose top priority was to save their vehicle. He ran into two Swiss students whose Land Rover developed some small problem, potentially serious, and they started back to Switzerland immediately. He tells of traveling part of the time with a group of Germans who abandoned their fairly new Peugeot car in the desert. They continued on their way, hitchhiking a ride on a truck. The most important thing to them was getting across the desert. The vehicle was just a means for getting there. Of course, there is something to admire in both mind-sets. Those people who headed back were certainly doing the prudent, responsible thing. The real difference is in terms of goals. Is the goal to preserve the vehicle, or to cross the desert?

I couldn't help but apply my son's discovery to this mission of rebuilding the church we have been talking about. Maintaining the vehicle, the buildings, the budget, the programs, the positions of power, can become all-consuming. We forget we're supposed to be going somewhere. That could even mean ditching the vehicle entirely and hitching a ride on the wings of the Spirit.

One snowy night in the deep woods, a field mouse was talking to a wild dove. It was one of those wonderful, windless nights with great, silent snowflakes falling.

"What are you doing?" asked the wild dove.

"I'm counting snowflakes," answered the mouse.

"What is the weight of a snowflake?"

"Nothing—nothing. The snowflake has no weight. But let me tell you something. I was sitting on a branch when the snow started, and I began to count the snowflakes that fell on my branch. I had counted 3,176,432, when, suddenly, one more snowflake fell and the whole branch broke."

In the same way, your voice may be the one to make a difference in the world. That one snowflake weighs less than nothing, but, added to what has gone before, a mighty branch may topple. That mission you feared was hopeless may turn out to be possible after all.

6. What About Miracles?

We cannot read the Exodus story without coming to grips with the whole subject of miracles, signs and wonders, unexplainable happenings that can be attributed only to the hand of God. Certainly the miracles of this particular story are among the best known to each and every Sunday school student. But miracles have been happening in all of the centuries since, some officially recorded, mostly by the Roman Catholic church, and others known only to faithful and grateful individual believers throughout the years.

What exactly constitutes a miracle? What puts any particular, unusual event in that category? Events considered miracles by the Jewish captives were seen as natural disasters by the Egyptians. That's a common problem in trying to sort out what is and isn't somehow the result of divine intervention. I was told about a young man who had been looking for work for many months. One morning he was on his way to what sounded like a promising job interview when he spotted a woman in distress along the road. Her car had a flat tire, and she was obviously in need of help. Being a Christian, he felt compelled to stop and offer assistance, even though that could mean being late for his important appointment.

He finally arrived at his destination and was ushered into the office of the personnel director. Behind the desk was the very same woman he had helped with the flat tire. It goes without saying that he got the job. You would call that a miracle—right? But, if you were one of the other job applicants that morning, you would probably describe what had happened as an unfortunate coincidence.

Some things we consider miraculous are simply the result of superior knowledge. For example, if you had told someone fifty years ago that it was possible to put a person on the moon, you'd be considered a certified "looney." Such a feat would seem to require supernatural powers. Today, we all know it can be done, although the technical intricacies of how it is done may escape us. It's no miracle.

A twenty-thousand-ton block of granite was found in the heart of the mountains of Peru. It is a single piece, and it rests over a half-mile from where it was quarried. No machinery in our modern-day world can move a rock that size, and yet it was transported by some means centuries ago. Does that constitute a miracle? And, assuming we discover how it was done, is it no longer miraculous?

A Connecticut Yankee in King Arthur's Court is Mark Twain's story of a modern man who finds himself back in the Middle Ages in the court of King Arthur. His superior knowledge makes him appear to be a miracle-worker, a wizard. At one point, when his life is at stake, he remembers that an eclipse is about to take place. "I have the power to blot out the sun," he boasts; and when his miracle occurs, his life is, of course, spared. He had a knowledge of the universe that his peers lacked, and it was considered miraculous.

As we said, there is a fine line between miracles and coincidences. The Bible speaks of time using two different Greek words—*kairos* and *chronos*. *Chronos* is measurable time, hours, days, weeks, years. *Kairos*, on the other hand, is the fullness of time, the moment of opportunity. We have all experienced those *kairos* times when circumstances just come together and produce some result we have been hoping and praying for. In some mysterious way, everything has been prepared. We simply do our part, and it all falls in place. Is it a miracle, or a mysterious coincidence?

The New Testament records that an earthquake occurred while Peter was in prison, and a second one later on, when Paul was imprisoned. Each time the earthquake was used to effect their release. Were those earthquakes the result of God's direct intervention, or did the earth tremors just happen to occur at the right time in the right place to bring about the deliverance of two of God's great apostles?

A very remote theory is used to explain the parting of the Red Sea as it is described in Exodus. Once, thousands of years ago, a volcano erupted on the Greek island of Santorini and touched off a huge tidal wave, wiping out all civilization on the island of Crete. That eruption could have occurred at just about the same time in history when the Israelites were fleeing the Egyptians. They were able to cross the Red Sea during its dry period, but this unexpected tidal wave of water broke just as the Egyptians attempted to follow. So far, that's an unsubstantiated theory. But, suppose it had happened that way? Would that timely coincidence make the destruction of Pharaoh's army any less a miracle?

Jesus, of course, did many miracles—most of them in the area of physical, mental and spiritual healing. We could wonder if that was the result of any special training. Some scholars suggest that Jesus may have studied briefly with the Essenes of the Qumram community, who were skilled in medical, scientific, and psychological arts. Personally, I am convinced Jesus was able to perform all kinds of miracles because He had access to the mind of God and a knowledge that transcended our finite understanding of His laws.

Norman Cousins, in his book *The Anatomy of an Illness*, emphasizes the therapeutic power of joy. Joy is salubrious and has positive, life-giving effects. When those who are ill learn how to laugh, celebrate, and rejoice, endorphins are released by the body. These positive substances help the body to combat diseased cells and tissues. They get well. That may be a natural phenomenon, but it's also miraculous.

I met a doctor at a Christian Medical Society meeting a few years ago on the East Coast. He had served as a missionary doctor in Africa and he told me about a miracle he had witnessed. Once, while working in a rural area, he treated a native from a neighboring village, a blacksmith whose arm was badly broken. The bone seemed totally destroyed. The arm was set and put in a cast and the man was advised to come back in six weeks.

Just two days later, the physician was driving through this same village and went by the blacksmith's shop. His patient was wielding a hammer and pounding on the forge. The cast was off. The doctor, horrified, jumped out of his jeep to put a stop to this folly. "No, no," protested the patient, "I am well. You made me well." Sure enough, the arm seemed healed. "How do you explain that?" asked my new friend. "I don't," I said. "I can't." Did the blacksmith's faith in the doctor make the bones mend instantly? Was it a genuine miracle, or some unusual case of mind over matter?

As we delve more and more into this area of healing, spiritual or physical, it is helpful to keep in mind that most illnesses have a termination point. In time, short or long, your immune system begins to work again, and you get well. In some cases, you get well without any treatment at all. You may attribute your recovery to prayers or to medical treatment, when actually the illness has simply run its course. As a counselor, I see a good many people who are suffering from depression. They are often the most sensitive and conscientious among us. I try to give them hope. In my experience, all depression has a termination point. It will not continue indefinitely. Recovery, whenever it eventually occurs, is sure to seem miraculous—and it is, in the sense that all healing is ultimately God's doing.

Miracles seem to require faith. The woman with the issue of blood touched Jesus' garment, and the illness she had suffered for years, and which doctors could not alleviate, was gone. Sir William Ousler, dean of North American medicine, once said to his students, "I am convinced that most of the people we heal get well because they have faith in our faith in the cure. We need new cures because we doctors lose our faith in the old cures."

In addition to joy and faith, there is another ingredient in those healing miracles we've been talking about, and that is hope. We are being told that when we come to the point where we believe we are going to get well, whether through medical treatment or a healing service or private prayers, the mind triggers production of interferon, which battles illness within the body. This natural drug is already in place and is released when needed.

The power to perform miracles can be attributed to at least three major sources. One is magic. The magicians of Pharaoh's court were able to reproduce some of Moses' and Aaron's miracles. Their magic was a matter of deception, sleight of hand, trickery. As a boy, I was fascinated with magic. Between the ages of seven and twelve, I spent all of my allowance buying magic tricks, and all of my time perfecting them and performing them for hapless dinner guests. I thought I was acquiring real power.

One of my favorite tricks was to pour clear water into an empty glass, say some magic words, and have the water suddenly turn blood red. Perhaps that's why I'm not surprised to read that when Moses turned the waters of the Nile into blood, the magicians could do that too. Moses and Aaron produced frogs, and so did the magicians. For some obscure reason, they could not reproduce the gnats. Certainly, many miraculous phenomena can be reproduced, but those Egyptian magicians soon came to realize that the signs and wonders they were witnessing were beyond trickery and deception.

The second obvious source of miraculous power is Satan himself. He promises power to those who will serve him rather than God, and, to a large extent, he can deliver. That is the premise of the Faustian legend. Satan makes a deal with Faust. "If you will give me your soul, I will give you whatever you want." It's a bargain he's been making through the ages. He tried it with Jesus during those forty days in the wilderness. We find Satan tempting Jesus in three separate areas. First of all, he would have his physical needs met. Turning the stones into bread would be just the first step down that particular path. The second was a chance to grab instant fame by a spectacular act of derring-do. He could throw himself off the pinnacle of the Temple and remain unharmed and wow the crowd.

The third temptation was Satan's trump card. Jesus could have it all—fame, power, and riches. According to Matthew's gospel, "the devil took him to a very high mountain and showed him all the kingdoms of the world and their splendor. 'All this I will give you,' he said, 'if you will bow down and worship me.'" In each case, Jesus refuted the temptations by quoting Old Testament scripture. In answer to that last offer, Jesus replied, "'Worship the Lord your God, and serve him only'" (Matthew 4:8–10). That was apparently Satan's undoing, and he left.

Then there is that third source of miraculous power, God Himself. Many of us have had firsthand experience of that power in our own lives and in the lives of friends and relatives. We can recount tales of healed bodies, healed relationships that seem explainable only in terms of divine intervention or a faith climate.

One such incident happened more than twenty years ago on my first trip to the Holy Land. Our group of sixty-five travelers included at least one skeptic, a psychiatrist from Oregon. At each stop in our pilgrimage, he seemed to enjoy playing devil's advocate—until the day when we reached the banks of the Jordan River. It was still a wild and lonely place in those days, and members of the group scattered, some to wade in the waters, others to sit quietly on the shores and meditate. Our skeptic took me aside. "Bruce," he began rather shyly, "I've had an open lesion on my leg for several years now, and it doesn't heal. I don't believe the Jordan has any magical properties, but the Bible records that God once healed a leper here. Would you be willing to pour some water on my leg right now and pray for me?"

I did, of course, but I didn't know if those prayers had availed anything until a week later. We were on the return trip, about to land at JFK, when I found my friend—we'll call him Frank—

standing in the aisle next to me. "I want you to see something," he said, and hiked up his pant leg. The lesion was gone. I have no idea if that experience ever turned him into a believer, but it affected my life in a special way. Just two years later, I was again on the banks of the Jordan with another group of pilgrims. I had been troubled for a year or more with a bleeding wart on my wrist that resisted healing. The next step seemed obvious. I splashed river water over my hand and wrist with this prayer, "Lord, you did it for Frank. Can you do it for me?" In a matter of days, the wart was gone, never to return.

That's one of those somewhat spooky stories that we feel almost embarrassed about, but it happened, and it leaves me convinced that God continues to do miracles. Sometimes, as with Frank, in the "test case" setting, and more often in response to the fervent prayers of the faithful. Certainly miracles come in assorted categories. The healing of a wart is not in the same category as the healing of a terminal cancer. The destruction of the whole Egyptian army with a tidal wave is a spectacular kind of miracle, but quieter miracles are taking place from time to time without fanfare and they go unrecognized. We might wonder about the purpose of miracles, since we will all die ultimately—healed or not. I think they are simply meant to produce belief and trust, love and obedience. The end product is a relationship with God Himself.

Pharaoh's hardness of heart in the face of all that had happened seems as miraculous to us as anything else. Even his magicians finally say, "This is the finger of God." But Pharaoh will not listen. Even God cannot penetrate his heart, and He cannot forcibly penetrate yours or mine. We can remain unbelievers as long as we choose to, to death and beyond. Our own unbelief is the ultimate power that we have over God. Pharaoh says he wants proof from Moses that this God of his exists, when his own heart should have condemned him for his acts of hatred and oppression against the Israelites.

We realize that he acted out of fear, a fear of this burgeoning slave population with its strange god and strange customs. He must have been convinced that their revolt was imminent, and therefore the persecutions and the genocidal policies (in the case of the male infants) were all justified. It's a rationale of all repressive governments.

Michael Walzer, a Jewish professor at Princeton University has written a book entitled *Exodus and Revolution.* He refutes the idea of a literal exodus during which these miracles took place. He interprets the book, instead, as a plan for social revolution, and, of course, social revolution in our politically uncertain world is a timely and compelling subject. Ryszard Kapuscinski, a Pole, wrote about the revolution in Iran, and his words would apply, I believe, to all revolutions.

> In every revolution, a movement grapples with structure, trying to destroy it, while the structure defends itself and tries to extinguish the movement. . . . The properties of a movement are spontaneity, impulsiveness, dynamic expansiveness and a short life. The properties of a structure are inertia, resilience and an amazing, almost instinctive ability to survive . . . Structures tend toward a return to the status quo, which they regard as the best of states, the ideal. This trait belies the inertia of the structure . . . A structure can also act like a roly poly toy. Just when it seems to have been knocked over, it pops back up.

Doesn't that description fit Pharaoh? He's knocked over again and again, but he pops back up and keeps popping back up to defend his kingdom. Kapuscinski is warning us that it is almost impossible to knock over an established structure. The miracle is that God through Moses took on the most powerful nation in the world of his time, and the revolution was successful. Defeated and desperate, Pharaoh finally let God's people go.

Whatever you make of miracles, or however you define them, the most significant miracle is the one that takes place in the human heart in response to God's relentless efforts to deliver us. There is something of Pharaoh in each one of us. How do we overcome our own hardness of heart? Hell is the state of being right at all cost. We say, "I was never wrong. I will not change." Our defensive self-righteousness leads to isolation and alienation.

A friend in Texas wrote me about the suicide of a nineteen-year-old boy, the son of close friends at church. He shared a copy of the suicide note with me. It said in part that he would rather die than ask for help. He would rather die than take a long, hard look at himself and expose his weakness to another person. He would rather die than change his mind and ask God for help. As extreme as that attitude seems, I don't think it's uncommon. The miracle is that you can continue to live that way for the rest of your life. It took miracle upon miracle to change Pharaoh's heart. Often it takes a miracle to change ours.

The doctrine of original sin is an important part of the Reformed tradition. If I had any questions about its truth, parenting has laid them to rest. With few exceptions, we come into the world howling for what we want, expecting to be the center of attention, making sure we get our fair share and more, exhibiting very little natural charity toward peers and less toward our siblings. We grow up and become more sophisticated in getting what we want, but we are still looking out for Number One with little inclination to sacrifice anything for needier members of the human family.

In that context, we begin to understand our need for a Redeemer, for a transformation that begins the quest for righteousness and justice for all people. That kind of change is a miracle—a lasting, world-changing revolution of the heart.

7. Deliverance

Those of you with Jewish friends and neighbors are familiar with the Seder feast. This is a meal celebrating the Passover, recounted in the eleventh and twelfth chapters of Exodus, and is central to the Jewish faith. The mandate for this high and holy day is found in these words: "And when your children ask you, 'What does this ceremony mean to you?' then tell them, 'It is the Passover sacrifice to the Lord, who passed over the houses of the Israelites in Egypt and spared our homes when he struck down the Egyptians'" (Exodus 12:26–27). Along with the expectation of a Messiah, this miraculous event was and continues to be the central hope of God's chosen people. God remembered them. God delivered them.

God, through Moses, gave detailed instructions about the Passover. Each household was to take a lamb without blemish and, on the evening of the fourteenth day, it was to be killed. Some of the blood must be sprinkled over the sides and tops of the door frames of each house. That blood would save them from death. The lamb was to be prepared and eaten a certain way. God's requirements were many and precise and they were followed.

For the last time, Pharaoh was warned by Moses of the horror to come—and what a horror. The firstborn son of every household, including Pharaoh's, was to be killed, as were the firstborn of all the cattle. Pharaoh is unmoved and, again, "his heart is hardened," and I, for one, have a hard time with that. Think of the lives that might have been saved had Pharaoh acquiesced at that point.

The events of that fateful night are described in terrible detail. "At midnight the Lord smote all the firstborn of the land of

Egypt, from the firstborn of Pharaoh who sat on his throne to the firstborn of the captive who was in the dungeon and all the firstborn of the cattle." Pharaoh and all the Egyptians rose in the night to discover this carnage, and "there was a great cry in Egypt, for there was not a house where one was not dead." Remember, this was a tropical land where, most likely, doors and windows were all open. We can only imagine the tens of thousands, even millions of agonized cries. What a sound that must have been!

Pharaoh summoned Moses and Aaron by night to say what I am sure that he passionately wished he had said long before, "Rise up, go forth from among my people, both you and the people of Israel; and go serve the Lord, as you have said. Take your flocks and your herds, as you have said, and be gone." And his last words are especially poignant: "And bless me also."

This great multitude of six hundred thousand men on foot, and the women and children and their flocks and herds, were at long last leaving. And, as he promised, God guided them, "By day the Lord went ahead of them in a pillar of cloud to guide them on their way and by night in a pillar of fire to give them light, so that they could travel by day or night" (Exodus 13:21). But they had scarcely departed when Pharaoh regrets his decision and wants his slaves returned.

The Israelites arrive at the edge of the Red Sea and, looking back, find Pharaoh and his entire army in pursuit. Their faithless and ungrateful reaction must have been a jolt to Moses. It was an indication of their slave mentality, an attitude he would be confronted with many times before their long sojourn ended. "They said to Moses, 'Was it because there were no graves in Egypt that you brought us away to the desert to die in the wilderness? What have you done to us, bringing us out of Egypt? Didn't we say, to you in Egypt, leave us alone; and let us serve the Egyptians? It would have been better for us to serve the Egyptians than to die in the desert.'"

Moses' reply is good advice for all of us, at times of doubt and anxiety. He says, "Do not be afraid. Stand firm and you will see the deliverance the Lord will bring you today . . ." We all know what happened next. Of all the Old Testament Bible stories, it is perhaps the most familiar and most sensational. Moses raises his rod and the sea divides and the people move through on dry land. They are miraculously delivered. Then, as the Egyptians begin to pursue, Moses raises his hand a second time. The water closes in, and the entire army is destroyed, "chariots, horsemen and all the host of Pharaoh." Then and only then do we find that "Israel saw the great work which the Lord did against Egypt, and people feared the Lord; they believed in the Lord and in his servant, Moses."

The formula for faith never varies. We are to fear not, stand firm, and expect God to deliver us from our enemies. We all have Egyptians pursuing us in some shape or form—internally or externally. We are sometimes unsure about the external enemies, but those internal ones of guilt, fear, addiction, and the rest are real enough. We all have at least two basic enemies. One is death. None of us will come out of this alive. Death is an unknown state and fear of the unknown is a universal fear. But God through the life, death, and resurrection of Jesus Christ has conquered death. He says, "Fear not, only believe. I am the resurrection and the life." We can stand firm and fear not. He will deliver us from that particular Egyptian.

Hell is another enemy in pursuit. Hell is not some future state. Hell is the now that never ends unless you experience the Lord's deliverance. We could describe it in hundreds of ways. Here are some of the personal hells many of us have been through:

- Hell is a jealousy that consumes you, that burns like a fire in your heart against those who have more than you do, and, furthermore, they don't deserve it.
- Hell is lust, lust for your neighbor's husband or wife, children, position, and possessions.
- Hell is anger—even justifiable anger, otherwise known as resentment.
- Hell is unforgiveness.

- Hell is self-doubt and self-hate that spirals into depression. We are convinced we are no good, worthless, defeated.
- Hell is an addiction to alcohol or drugs, or to negative, self-destructive behavior of any kind.

But however often we have knowingly broken God's law, His grace is available if we seek it. We do not earn our deliverance, even with a lifetime of good works. Jesus promised the thief on the cross and He promises us, "You shall be with me in paradise."

For the believer, those enemies—death and hell—are already destroyed. The first step of faith is to appropriate that promise. The Israelites were saved by the blood of the Lamb, and so are we. The Bible says over and over and over again that there is no remission of sin apart from the shedding of blood. We are not saved by our good works, or by our good nature. We are not saved by our generosity or our loving attitude. We are saved by the blood of the Paschal Lamb, Jesus Christ.

Think, if you will, of the meanest, most obnoxious individual you know. You can say to that person with perfect honesty, "Friend, Jesus died for you." Of course, we have to appropriate that atonement for ourselves to be redeemed, forgiven, but it is still accurate to tell the most heinous sinner, "Jesus shed His blood for you. You are loved."

Throughout Vachel Lindsey's poem "General Booth Enters Heaven," this refrain is repeated again and again, "Are you washed in the blood of the Lamb?" It is a stirring work, and it always moves me, but on the other hand, there are many corny hymns about the blood of the Lamb that are offensive, both musically and theologically. But that doesn't change the fact that our only hope of life now and forever rests in the blood of Jesus Christ.

There is a paradox about belief. Belief means acting as if it were true *before* we believe. When God was obeyed, when the blood was displayed over the doorpost, all Jewish households were spared. They might have been skeptical, but they acted in faith as God directed. A young preacher once came to John Wesley claiming he had lost his faith. How could he find it again? "Go out and preach until you get it," he was told. The Israelites followed God's instructions scrupulously while still uncertain of the outcome and God's ability to deliver them. Faith is acting as if the good news is true in your life. That means we are to relax, to stop worrying, to claim God's love and presence and trust His ability to deliver us. Our enemies are already defeated. We can live life at a slower pace. We can live life as though God were in control, whether we believe that at the moment or not.

Igor Stravinsky, one of the great musicians and composers of our time, was once asked by his publisher to hurry up and get a particular work completed. He said, "I'm sorry. My life is so full, I have no time to hurry." That's not a bad way for you and me to live our lives, to believe that God can deliver us from the tyranny of time, as well as from the tyranny of our anxieties and our passions.

The Israelites were delivered, first because they acted in faith, and second because they followed God's rules. The rules of the Passover meal, as we said, were to be strictly followed. We might say they were a forerunner of the precise rules to come later on through the Ten Commandments.

Naaman, the mighty man who had leprosy, found he had to follow God's rules, distasteful as they were. He came to the prophet, Elisha, seeking healing. His own magicians and physicians were unable to cure him. He was told to go wash in the Jordan River seven times. He was astonished and skeptical, saying, in effect, "That stinking river? With all of the clean, sparkling rivers in my own land, why must I bathe there?" But he followed God's precise rules laid out through Elisha, and he was healed.

I had dinner recently with an unusual woman who had been trying to live out obedient discipleship and follow God's rules for many years. She had a strange story to tell about how God first broke into her life. It seems she met some Christians at a very sophisticated dinner party and they were talking about giving God your life and trying to find His guidance every day. She decided to do that. The very next morning she was praying, "Lord, I want to be your person. What do you want me to do today?" The words that came to mind seemed absurd. "Clean out your dresser drawers." "I expected something more spiritual," she confessed. "But those drawers were a mess. They somehow symbolized all the clutter in my life at that time. That act was the beginning of obedience for me. I'm still trying to find God's will and do it."

Which leads us to the third ingredient in the deliverance of the Israelites. They let God guide them. We now have the Ten Commandments, the Sermon on the Mount, the Beatitudes; but even with those marvelous, life-giving rules, we have to let God guide us. The Israelites making their way in the wilderness never had to agonize over whether or not they were guided. The signs were clearly visible—a pillar of cloud by day and a pillar of fire by night. Since Pentecost, we have something just as dramatically present in our lives to guide us—the Holy Spirit, the wind and fire of God's own Spirit is in the breast of every believer. You know when that Spirit is speaking. At a crucial time, you feel prompted to make that visit, call this friend, take that new job, write a letter, ask forgiveness.

By my time of life, you'd think I would have learned that it is imperative to follow God's leading. Recently, I took an overnight trip to the East Coast, which turned out to be a disaster in every way. Coming back I had a chance to reflect and do some serious praying. I said, "Lord, why did this happen?" The answer came clearly. I had felt from the outset that I was not supposed to make that trip. Why did I go anyway? I had wasted two days of my time and somebody else's money. "Lord," I prayed, "you tried to guide me about this trip, and I shouldn't have gone. Help me be more obedient in the future."

Some of the guidance God gave the Israelites seems unusual. "Ask the Egyptians for their gold and silver." I'm not surprised that the Egyptians handed it over. They were terrified and eager to be done with these troublemakers. But even that transaction was an important part of God's larger plan. Those resources would be crucial to their survival in the ensuing years. It may help to remember that part of the Exodus story the next time you have to ask people for money for a good cause.

I heard about a couple who had a man arrive on their doorstep one afternoon asking for a donation. "A family down the street is in desperate trouble," he explained. "The father is out of work, the kids are hungry, the landlord is about to evict them this very afternoon, unless they can come up with the rent money. Can you help?" "You bet! We'd be glad to," was the response. "By the way, who are you?" "I'm the landlord," was the answer. Concern, in that case, was prompted by self-interest; but, in the best sense, all philanthropy is motivated by self-interest. By our gifts we bless and enrich our own lives. We need to be bolder about hitting up our Egyptian neighbors, meaning those uncommitted, happy pagans all around us, for some good and godly cause—street kids, food banks, famine relief, whatever. Most of us are a little embarrassed. I feel less so as the years go on. I realize that people need an opportunity to share in God's work throughout the world, and that those gifts will bless the givers even more than they will the recipients.

I can't help but think that our attitude toward money is a real barometer of our faith in God. The famous Good Samaritan story is about charity and the lack of it, but it also reveals three basic attitudes that we have about money.

The first is, "What's yours is mine." That's the attitude of the robbers who stripped the traveler, beat him, and left him half dead. Then we could say that the priest and Levite who passed by without helping were "what's mine is my own" types. They were too concerned with themselves and their own affairs to have compassion for the injured man. Finally there's the Good Samaritan. He seems to feel "what's mine is yours," and he exemplifies the attitude we come to as we realize that all we have and are is God's gift to us. His time, his energy, and his personal resources were all at the disposal of the injured man.

When it comes to possessions, we need to keep in mind that none of us actually own anything. Our houses, cars, stocks, cash, all will some day belong to somebody else. Those things are simply ours for a time. Only the soul is eternal. The body is left behind to decay.

But our concern for that body can extend beyond the grave. That was the case with the patriarch Joseph. He had extracted a deathbed oath from the sons of Israel that his bones would be taken back to his homeland. So it was that, in addition to the gold and silver of the Egyptians, the Israelites carried one more precious item out of their place of bondage—Joseph's bones. His request was honored and eventually those bones were buried at Shechem on a tract of land that Jacob bought from the sons of Hamor.

When God delivers you from death—which He has—and from hell—which He can and will—take the best of the old with you. In the case of the Israelites, it was the bones of Joseph, a symbol of the great days of the past. I urge you to do the same as you move out to your personal promised land. Take all the best of your early training and nurturing, of your experience and education, of your relationships and memories.

Fear not, stand firm, and see the salvation of the Lord.

8. The Price of Freedom

The life of faith is a journey. It is movement, and that is why the Exodus, this saga of the departure from Egypt and the subsequent wanderings, is so pertinent to your life and mine. We find the Israelites moving from bondage into freedom, but they do not do so happily. That seems a little strange, but, upon closer examination, we realize their behavior is a reflection of our own.

God's great ultimate gift for all of us is freedom, and yet something in us resists that gift. You could say we have something of a death wish, to put it in pyschological terms. We are constantly tempted to go back to old habits, old attitudes, old sins. The old bondage looks attractive once more. We are not always eager to claim the new thing God has for us. We fight God, and out of His love, He contends with us and will not let us go. He insists, as He did with the Israelites, that "you are my people."

As we read about the events after the destruction of the Egyptian army, we are astonished that God did not give up on those querulous, faithless wanderers. Just three days after that miraculous deliverance, they are wandering in the desert and they are thirsty, these several million people and their cattle. They arrive at an oasis only to find that the water is bitter, and they do what they continue to do whenever they are faced with a crisis. They murmur against Moses and Aaron. Actually, they are murmuring against God, but they don't quite dare to do that openly. God directs Moses to toss a certain branch on the water, and immediately those bitter waters become sweet and drinkable.

We might assume that witnessing that miracle would have some lasting effect, but it didn't. A month and a half later we find them wandering in the southwest Sinai desert, and they are murmuring again. They were hungry. They missed the pots of meat they used to have in Egypt. Killing their cattle and goats was not an option. A nomadic people on the move needed those animals for milk and cheese and all the related dairy products. In memory, they ate so well back in Egypt. That seems unlikely. Slave people then or now do not eat well. I have a hunch it's like remembering mom's cooking. In our minds, it was great, the best. Sometimes we go home as adults and find it isn't so great after all. All those meat loaves and jello salads have lost their charm. The Israelites may have been having the same kind of sentimental recollections—those pots of meat were so savory, so delicious, and here they are with no meat and no bread. Moses has brought them into the desert to starve.

God acts once again to deliver them. They are to go out each morning and gather manna. Manna is thought to be a kind of edible hoarfrost. Research has proven that a pound of this high-carbohydrate substance each day is enough to live on. The miracle is that several million people could gather enough of this substance to survive forty long years. The word *manna* means literally, "what is it?" They ate "what is it?" for the next four decades. That took care of their need for bread, but what about meat? A sudden and powerful wind manages to blow millions of quail onto the desert. According to the text "they covered the camp."

Sometimes it's a scary thing when God gives us what we want. There is a permissiveness in God that is frightening, especially for us parents. Jesus told the story of the Prodigal Son who asked for his share of the inheritance to go into the far country. In today's terms, we might say he was seeking self-actualization. The father, well aware of the son's proclivity for high living and self-indulgence, lets him go and finances the trip. So it was with the Israelites; their demands were met. They got both bread and meat.

There was a condition, however, regarding the manna. They

were to gather only enough each day, and no more. Some disobeyed, of course, and gathered more, only to find it full of maggots the next day. On the sixth day they were to gather a double portion. Those who didn't went out on the seventh day and found none.

Isn't it amazing that with only two simple rules about gathering manna, there were still those who wanted to bend those rules. The first two people, Adam and Eve, were given just one rule: Don't eat from a particular tree. Eve, after a conversation with the serpent, was determined to bend that rule. You and I don't like rules, no matter how few, and that is a part of our problem.

God continued to supply the needs of that desert band, and don't you think that in His heart and mind He was hoping that they would eventually learn to trust Him? He had destroyed their enemies, turned bitter water to sweet, and provided bread and meat. When would they stop murmuring and believe that He would take care of them? The shocking part of it all is that we are those people. So much of the time, we are just like those faithless, skeptical Israelites.

From time to time I counsel people who are in some terrible situation and who see no way out. They don't believe God can deliver them. I like to remind them how far they have come. "Look at all the problems you have faced up to now. You're a survivor. There was a time when you were one of three million sperm racing up a birth canal to unite with an egg, and you beat out all the other contenders. You are a survivor from the beginning, and you keep on surviving. Bad things may have happened to you, but you're still here. Why doubt God at this point in your pilgrimage?" That pep talk seems to help in most cases.

The Israelites couldn't handle their new freedom, and that is a problem we can identify with. Freedom is always costly and more than a little frightening. We listen, instead, to those voices within clamoring for security and comfort. When we have no more needs or anxieties, freedom will be a byproduct. Freedom is never a byproduct. Freedom is a direct gift of God.

The founding fathers of our nation suffered from religious oppression in Europe and came here to pursue freedom. They did not come to pursue job security or adequate pensions or comprehensive health plans or to have no anxieties. If anything, their anxieties multiplied. But they understood that pursuing God's gift of freedom was worth the risk. Dostoyevski's brilliant work, *The Brothers Karamazov*, is set during the time of the Inquisition. In a powerful scene, Jesus himself has returned in the flesh, and the grand inquisitor speaks to Him about freedom in this amazing speech:

> Thou hast made us free and thou respecteth our freedom, but who told thee we want to be free? We prefer to be slaves, provided we be secure and we enjoy ourselves. Freedom is too onerous a burden to bear. Away with it! Who wants to choose for himself? Who wants to be responsible? Let others choose and be responsible for us. All we want is security and pleasure. Thou hast thought that we are gods like thyself, but we are no gods at all. We are corrupt human beings. Thy love for us is misplaced. Thy gift to us is unwanted. Thou hast said, "Ye shall know the truth and the truth shall make you free," but we say with Pilate, "What is truth?" And we add, "Who cares to be free?"

Does the inquisitor speak for the whole human race? Perhaps. Something in us hungers for the stewpots of Egypt, the certain, the comfortable. That's more precious than the gift of freedom. What does it mean to yearn for the old comforts to you and me today in America? We yearn for job security. We want no pain or anxiety, and to cope we turn to alcohol and drugs. We give up our freedom in order to blot out our problems. That's at the heart of the appeal of the demagogue. They'll take care of us. They'll save us from our enemies. In return for our allegiance, we will be cared for and protected. It's so attractive. We can get rid of the troublesome burdens of freedom. We are comfortable in bondage.

My mother was. I've written about her often. She was a great servant of the Lord, and I owe my faith to her and her prayers.

But an unfortunate thing occurred when she was in her late eighties in a retirement home. She was widowed and lonely, and she began to take tranquilizers to the extent that she got hopelessly hooked on them. A fall put her in the hospital, where her supplies were not available, and she suffered agonizing withdrawal symptoms. A new doctor came on the scene, recognized her symptoms, and insisted she go cold turkey. She was cured, but she never forgave him. The previous doctor made her feel good, while this new man let her pain continue. Nevertheless, when she finally died at ninety-three, she was in her right mind and her full powers, delivered from the bondage of addiction.

We have an active Faith, Hope, and Recovery group meeting in our church every Sunday evening. As I have met with them and heard their stories, I am amazed at how many people are addicts because of prescription drugs given to them by trusted physicians. As a society, we are more and more unwilling to deal with pain and anxiety. A cartoon in a recent New Yorker magazine showed a psychiatrist walking out of his office with his arm around an obviously troubled man. The caption has him saying, "Yes, yes, indefinable cravings, sleeplessness and occasional outbursts of rage. It's just something that's going around." It's always been going around. That's the human condition.

God wants to give us freedom. If we turn back to painlessness, to comfort and security and safety, we're choosing death, now and forever. God has better things for us. Unfortunately, much of the time we're like the caterpillar, who watches a butterfly fly by and says to himself, "You'll never get me up in one of those things." God has a better dream for us than we can imagine. If we can shed our prison, our cocoon, we may even fly.

To do so, we may have to leave our comforts, and we are a comfortloving people. Our family tried camping just once when our three children were small. We bought a Volkswagen bus and a stove and a tent and drove all over the country for almost two months. We never went camping again. I like to tell my wife that her idea of roughing it is slow room service but, if I'm honest, I am as addicted as she is to the comfortable life. I might consider camping for a week, but mainly I want to be comfortable, and that addiction can interfere with God's dream for me.

The freedom God offers has two obvious dimensions. There is the freedom *from*. The Israelites were freed from their oppressors, free of Egypt, free from Pharaoh. But they were given the freedom to *become*, free to claim the land and live a new way as God's servant people. Freedom *from* is just the first step. Martin Luther has stated the paradox so well: "The Christian is the most free lord of all, subject to no one. A Christian is the most dutiful servant of all, subject to everyone." As we find our bondage to Jesus, we are free from the hindering, binding things of the world, but we are free, then, to become His disciples, His agents of change in the world.

There are many wonderful Lincoln stories, but one of my favorites concerns an incident that took place in his White House years during the Civil War. He didn't go to church regularly on Sunday because his presence might cause a fuss, but he often slipped out to the Wednesday night service at the New York Avenue Presbyterian Church. The pastor, Dr. Gurley, was asked to leave his study door open so that Lincoln could come in that way and hear the service from that secluded place.

On one such night, an aide came along. On the return walk, he asked the president how he liked the sermon. "I thought it was well-thought through, powerfully delivered and very eloquent," was the reply. "Oh," continued the aide, "you thought it was a great sermon." "No," said Lincoln, "it failed. It failed because Dr. Gurley did not ask us to do something great." Any authentic message about God and His will for us ought to leave no doubt that there is something great required of us.

There is another lesson about freedom in the story of the manna. God's people were to gather sustenance daily. This amazing honeylike substance, full of carbohydrates and nutrients, would keep them alive. But they were to take one day's supply at a time, except on the sixth day. Our freedom requires a daily dependence upon God. Without that daily guidance, power, infilling, we're going to go back to the old life of bondage. That grace is supplied anew every day. There are no shortcuts. We can't buy indulgences for future missteps. We can't collect grace and save it for a rainy day. One Alcoholics Anonymous slogan is, "One day at a time." Nothing can happen in one day that you and I can't, with God's presence and help, handle. If we take our freedom for granted and start planning for years ahead, we're going to fail.

Finally, we can't make the faith journey alone. We need help and support from our other brothers and sisters on the journey. Even Moses had to come to that realization. It happened this way. Apparently, Moses had sent his wife, Zipporah, to tell her father, Jethro, that the Lord had blessed his mission and that he was in the vicinity of Mount Sinai. Jethro came to visit and hear all the great things that God had done.

The next day, however, Jethro watched as people lined up outside of Moses' tent from sunup to sundown, waiting for him to solve their problems and judge their disputes. He asked a pointed question: Why do you alone sit as judge? Moses tries to explain that, among other things, he informs them of God's decrees and laws. His father-in-law gives him some straight talk. "What you are doing is not good. You and these people who come to you will only wear yourselves out. The work is too heavy for you. You cannot handle it alone. Listen now to me, and I will give you some advice." He goes on to outline an ingenious plan. Choose trustworthy, God-fearing men and appoint them as judges over thousands, hundreds, fifties, and tens. Let them refer difficult cases to Moses, but decide the simpler ones themselves. Let others share the load. We could say that Jethro was an organizational genius and more. He hit upon the secret of kingdom-building in any age. That, friends, was the birth of the small-group movement.

The leader who has genuine authority does not need to be

authoritative. Authoritative people who need to hold all of the reins of power are doing a disservice to themselves and everyone else. Good leadership is shared leadership. The death of Prime Minister Nehru created a leadership vacuum in India. It was said that he was like a great banyan tree under which many took shelter but nothing grew. Jesus shared leadership with the twelve disciples. They were sent out two by two to preach and teach and heal. He didn't even go along on those occasions. I'm sure Jethro's concept of leadership was revolutionary in that time, but in it we see something of the mind of God for the affairs of His church. His Spirit dwells in each of us and together we are to build the Kingdom, supporting and encouraging each other.

It is a credit to Moses that he immediately heeded Jethro's advice. He was not defensive or threatened. The concept of shared leadership is put into practice. The people begin to act as priests to one another, and Moses' job is, at last, manageable.

The price of freedom then is costly, risky living. We move beyond our need for security and comfort, we let God feed us day by day with His holy bread, and we practice a leadership style marked by humility and eagerness to share authority and power with our teammates and companions of the way.

Risky living is the bottom line of the faith journey. I was given an anonymous piece recently that puts it this way:

> To laugh is to risk appearing the fool. To weep is to risk appearing sentimental. To reach out for another is to risk involvement. To expose feelings is to risk exposing your true self. To place your ideas, your dreams, before the crowd is to risk their loss. To love is to risk not being loved in return. To live is to risk dying. To hope is to risk despair. To try is to risk failure. But, risks must be taken because the greatest hazard in life is to risk nothing. The person who risks nothing does nothing, has nothing, and is nothing. He may avoid suffering and sorrow, but he simply cannot learn, feel, change, grow and love and live. Chained by his certitudes, he is a slave. He has forfeited freedom. Only a person who risks is free.

II. GOD THE GUIDE

9. God's Dream for Us

Occasionally, we sing a hymn in our worship services entitled, "How I Love Thy Law, O Lord." The law refers, of course, to the Ten Commandments. The last time I heard the congregation singing that lustily, I began to wonder about the truth of it. How many of us are crazy about the Ten Commandments? We should be but, more often than not, we ignore them or try to find ways to bend them. We hate being confronted by our failures and shortcomings.

Recently, in the midst of a heated discussion, a close friend asked a pertinent question. "Do you want me to tell you what's wrong with you?" I thought a moment and said, "No, not really." As a Christian I'm supposed to be committed to growing, to becoming more than I am. When someone offers to point out what's wrong with me, I ought to be glad to be shown those places where I'm sinning and falling short of the mark. Surely that is the essential purpose of the law. It reveals the style of life God had in mind for us from the beginning, the rules to maximize our relationships to Him and to each other.

The law, meaning the Ten Commandments found in the twentieth chapter of Exodus, was given to Moses at Mount Sinai. The Israelites were three months along in their journey, a journey marked by the miraculous providence of God—daily manna, quail, bitter water made sweet, water gushing from a rock. They had made camp in the desert of Sinai at the foot of the mountain.

Interestingly, the location of Mount Sinai where God gave the law has never been clearly established. The rabbis, who in later years spent their lives sorting through the many and minute laws given there, cared not at all about where Mount Sinai was. A search for the exact spot was not initiated until the fourth century *a.d.*, when Constantine's mother undertook her quest to find the holy places. In my view, the rabbis had the right idea. What matters is *what* happened, not *where* it happened. The law is to be revered, not the mountain where it was given.

On that historic morning, there was thunder and lightning and thick clouds hovering over the summit. The voice of the Lord called Moses to the top. An elaborate plan for crowd control had been worked out in advance, and the people were kept at a distance. God sent for Aaron as well, and the law was then laid out for the two leaders. The book of Exodus devotes the next eleven chapters to the laws given Moses and Aaron on that occasion, laws dealing with every part of Hebrew life—their worship, their social responsibilities, even detailed plans for the tabernacle and the Ark of the Covenant. But for our purposes here, when we speak of the law, we mean the Ten Commandments; and we will be exploring those in depth in these next chapters.

Our feelings about the law depend largely on our relationship to God. Who is our God and what is His nature? For some, God is like a state trooper. State troopers serve an important function, but most of us are not happy to see them behind us on the freeway suddenly blowing their sirens and flashing their lights. I think a good many people feel God is following them down the freeway of life, waiting for one slip and eager to say, "I gotcha! Pull over. You're in big trouble." That's not the God we find in either Old or New Testaments, and it is certainly not the God revealed in the Ten Commandments. I would compare that God to a commander in the Coast Guard. He wants to help you get your boat out of the shoals and treacherous reefs and into safe waters. He has put up ten black and red markers to make sure we stay in the channel. Even if we get out of the channel (and all of us do) we still know how to get back to it because of those markers. In that context, we see that the law is a gift from a loving God who is our friend.

One of my favorite verses is James 2:23: "'Abraham believed God, and it was credited to him as righteousness', and he was called God's friend." Abraham left the channel on more than one occasion. He doubted and he was disobedient, but he knew where the channel was, and that the God who had given him directions was his friend.

The author of Psalm 19 writes with such glowing love for the law and its life-giving properties: "The law of the Lord is perfect, reviving the soul. The statutes of the Lord are trustworthy, making wise the simple. The precepts of the Lord are right, giving joy to the heart. The commands of the Lord are radiant, giving light to the eye. The fear of the Lord is pure, enduring forever. The ordinances of the Lord are sure and altogether righteous."

Beyond providing eternal guidelines for the living of life, the law serves a second important purpose. It reveals to us the mind of the Creator. It is a window into the heart of the Lawgiver and His plans and purposes for us. Lacking that, we find ourselves easily distracted and diverted into lesser causes and trivial concerns. I heard about a teacher who sent the following note home with one of her students: "Your daughter excels in initiative, group integration, responsiveness, and activity-participation. Now, if she'd only just learn to read and write." We can all excel at many good and worthy things and miss the whole purpose of being. We can major in the minors, and the law reminds us of what God intends for us.

Even Albert Einstein, the premier scientist of this century, was intrigued to learn more about the mind of God, the nature of the Lawgiver. He wrote, "Science without religion is lame. Religion without science is blind. I want to know how God created this world. I'm not interested in this or that phenomenon and the spectrum of this or that element. I want to know His thoughts. The rest are details." Einstein is saying, of all things, that the purpose of science is to know the thoughts of God. The law is the revelation of those thoughts about us.

God's greatest gift is, of course, the gift of himself in Jesus Christ, and Jesus came, in His words, "to fulfill the law."

We see in these ten rules as they are recorded in Exodus a law that supercedes all other laws—federal, state, communal, even individual ethics and codes of behavior. Imagine, if you will, that a young lad comes to the city from a farm in Montana. He has spent all of his early years in a town of two or three hundred people, milking cows, feeding chickens, tending pigs. He is a believer and a churchgoer and he takes these commandments we have been talking about seriously. In the city he meets all kinds of people: punk rockers with multicolored hair and safety pins in their ears, culture buffs who know all about opera and concerts and art, politicians and business tycoons. But with his knowledge of God's laws, he has learned about truth and fidelity, honesty and love, sacrifice and commitment. He may know more about life than a good many of those sophisticated urbanites who understand only the now with no grasp of the eternal.

The law is not an end in itself. It represents the covenant God has made with us. He says, "Now, if you obey me fully and keep my covenant, then out of all nations you will be my treasured possession. Although the whole earth is mine, you will be for me a kingdom of priests, a holy nation" (Exodus 19:5–6). God has a dream for us. The law is meant to help us fulfill that dream. But keeping the law is not the ultimate goal. That is the error Israel fell into and does to this day. So many Orthodox Jews are intent on understanding the law, keeping the law, every jot and tittle of it. Volumes are written explaining, interpreting, examining. The law is God's good gift which sets forth the conditions of His covenant with us, but the result is to produce a royal priesthood. God's dream for His people, old and new covenant, is the same. We are to be a kingdom of priests, a holy nation.

The priesthood of all believers is a crucial doctrine in the Christian tradition, but the idea is awesome. Keep in mind, however, that a priest is someone who stands between God and another person as a link or a channel person. Personally, I think the process is a kind of spiritual mitosis. Most of us learn in biology that all life comes from previously existing life. A cell divides and life multiplies. At Pentecost, when the church was born, God's Spirit was let loose in the world through the believers present. That Spirit moved from person to person throughout the known world.

Every believer has a spiritual genealogy, whether he or she is aware of it or not. Perhaps you came to faith through Billy Graham's ministry, as so many people have. Your spiritual genealogy has already been researched in detail. In 1858, a Sunday school teacher named Kimball led a Boston shoe clerk to give his life to Christ. That clerk was Dwight Moody, who became an evangelist. In 1879, Moody preached in England and the Spirit claimed the heart of Frederick B. Myer, pastor of a small church. Myer, preaching on an American college campus, converted a student named J. Wilbur Chapman. Chapman, engaged in YMCA work, employed a former baseball player, Billy Sunday, to assist him in his evangelical campaigns. Sunday held a revival in Charlotte, North Carolina. As a result, a group of local citizens were so enthusiastic that they planned a second campaign with Mordecai Ham as the preacher.

In that second revival meeting, a young man named Billy Graham heard the gospel and gave his life to Christ. If Billy Graham led you to Christ, you can trace your genealogy back well over one hundred years to Mr. Kimball, the Sunday school teacher. Actually, every Christian has a genealogy that goes all the way back to Pentecost from person to person. That's the royal priesthood. I charge you to make sure it does not stop with you. Continue to introduce those around you to a God of grace, a God of glory, a God of love.

Let's see what the first commandment reveals about the mind and nature of that God. It is the one on which all the other nine depend. *You shall have no other gods before me*. Traditionally and historically, there have been three different concepts about God: polytheism, pantheism, and monotheism. Polytheism is the worship of many gods. Pantheists, though they believe there are many gods, choose one to worship and serve. Monotheism, for which the Jews were known from earliest times, is the belief that there is but one God in the world to be worshiped and served.

The Israelites had lived for generations among the Egyptians who had many gods. When this first commandment was given, God was well aware that they had many gods bidding for their attention. We still do. There are always those things that tend to become more important in your life and mine than God. Sometimes family concerns and interests take first place. As we examine our preoccupation with nutrition, exercise and health care, we could wonder if more and more of us aren't worshiping health or longevity.

A whole lot of other things can move, almost unnoticed, into that place before God—academic achievement, money, power, sex, drugs, alcohol. Your career may be your god and time and family and health will be sacrificed to that idol. Sometimes resentment is the thing that comes between us and God and moves Him to second place. Some people live to keep a grudge going. It is their reason for being. I heard about an old man who had held a grudge against his neighbor for many years. Ill and expecting to die, he called the neighbor to his bedside. "I want you to know I forgive you for what you did to me so many years ago," he said. "But, if I get well, the grudge still holds."

Anything in our life that seems to consume our total time and attention is a contender for God's place. When Jesus was asked about the most important commandment, He might have named any of the ten. "Don't lie, don't steal, don't commit adultery . . ." But He didn't. The first and greatest commandment is to put God above everything else in your life. The familiar verse, "Seek ye first the kingdom of God, and all the rest will be added unto you," is good advice, but I would amend it a little. "Seek ye first the kingdom of God, or forget about seeking it at all."

I am a great fan of John Wesley, founder of the Methodist church—his writings, his class meetings, his evangelical fervor. I am, in fact, a closet Methodist. He and so many of his followers were individuals passionately seeking first the Kingdom of God. One of his disciples was a preacher named John Nelson, whose preaching resulted in his imprisonment. He was considered an enemy of the state Church of England, and he was jailed for his faith. His cell was located beneath a slaughterhouse, and in his journal he wrote: "It stank worse than a pigsty because of the blood and filth that flowed into it from above. But my soul was so filled with the love of God that it was Paradise for me."

Few of us have been or are going to be in a slaughterhouse jail, but life might still seem to be a pigsty because of unhappy relationships or unfortunate, even tragic, circumstances. Even so, if God is number one, we can say as Paul did, "I have learned the secret of being content in any and every situation, whether well fed or hungry, whether living in plenty or in want. I can do everything through him who gives me strength" (Philippians 4:12–13).

Israel focused on the law and forgot the covenant. We who are the new Israel ignore the law often, or bend it, and forget the covenant. Our problem today, as someone said, is that we say, "Thou shalt not steal (much)"; "Thou shalt not commit adultery (unless you are deeply in love)"; "Thou shalt not bear false witness (unless you're in a jam)." We're like the individual in the automobile showroom who eyed the very sleek-looking car and asked, "What if some crazy nut should want to exceed the speed limit? What would this baby do?" Most of us occasionally do crazy things—exceed the speed limit and break the law. But it need not break us. God's grace is still operating. We can say, "Lord, I'm on the sand bank. I'm on the rocks. But I know where the channel is." Those markers are eternal and will guide us back into a covenant relationship God has planned for us.

10. A Nonportable God

The first four commandments zero in on our relationship to God and our duty toward Him. He is a jealous God and He demands total, wholehearted service. In the next six commandments, we find the rules for our relationship to each other—parents, neighbors, friends, strangers. The second commandment concerns the worship of idols. It starts with these words: "You shall not make for yourself an idol in the form of anything in heaven above or on the earth beneath or in the waters below" (Exodus 20:4).

The whole idea of idols, statues, graven images, seems to most of us in the Western world ridiculous. They were also ridiculous to the Old Testament prophets. Isaiah wrote scathingly about people who worshiped idols. He says they plant a tree, raise it up, and then chop it in three parts. One part is used to keep warm; another part provides fuel to cook food; and, with the last third, a statue is carved. To worship that part of the wood and call it "god" is ludicrous, according to Isaiah. Jeremiah compares idols to scarecrows in a cucumber patch. They are unable to move. In the event of fire, they must be rescued and carried to safety. They are unable to protect themselves. How, then, can they protect anyone else?

Personally, I find the distinction between the first and second commandments a little blurred for those of us in the twentieth century. The first commandment, when it was given, was a clear call to monotheism in a time when many gods were being worshiped. The second had to do with fashioning objects of wood, stone, metal, and then attributing to those objects the power to control our destinies. During the Middle Ages, the reformers accused the Roman church of doing that. They were convinced the statues, paintings, icons, were replacing God

Himself, and were being revered and worshiped in His place. We know some of the excesses to which they carried their zeal in this regard. In places where they eventually came to power, beautiful works of art were destroyed and, in some cases, whole cathedrals were razed. But for most of us, it's hard to distinguish between idols and other gods. For our purposes, I'd say that whatever has first place in your life and mine, anything or anyone which claims our allegiance and devotion has become our god or our idol.

Buddha, the revered teacher who never claimed to be a god, has nevertheless become, for some of his followers, both a god and an idol. I remember visiting a Buddhist shrine in Macau a few years ago. There was the usual obese, complacent, inward-looking statue, with worshipers burning incense and making obeisance to him. But another ceremony was taking place nearby, a funeral custom I was unfamiliar with.

The bereaved were clustered about a doll's house made of paper, mostly cardboard, and it was exquisitely constructed and lavishly furnished. It represented the house that the deceased family member would have in the next life. It contained television sets, stereo equipment, refrigerators, deep freezes, and telephones. There was even a paper Mercedes-Benz in the driveway. The palatial-looking house was crammed with all the things that the desperately poor people of Macau don't have. The house featured a picture of the dead person. This was all to be burned shortly in the belief that all these material possessions would follow the departed into the next world. In that life, they would have all of the luxuries they had missed in this one. We stayed long enough to observe the mourning family as the conflagration took place, and it was a heartbreaking sight. The best hope their idol offered was a future life with more of this world's goods.

There are many secular idols that promise much and capture our attention and, eventually, leave us unfulfilled and unsatisfied. We get some clues about their nature and variety as we observe our pagan neighbors on Sunday mornings, and see the things they are substituting for the worship of God. I see a lot of them polishing and waxing the car. Can the car really be an idol whose maintenance has us in its grip?

Even a house can be an idol. The house ought to exist to serve the family, but, in some cases, it seems the family exists to serve the house. We must all use it carefully, come in the back door, and eat only in the kitchen. We are endlessly vacuuming, scrubbing, polishing this object of our worship. A boat is a kind of idol—and I say this very cautiously, since I own one. I live in a city with a huge percentage of boat owners. You can visit our largest marina and see as many as two thousand idols at a crack, bobbing around. Unless you are a very wealthy person, a boat of any size can soon be your master. It will consume your money, your time, and your attention. We would be reluctant to call it worship, but that's a possibility.

We even have some living idols in our twentieth-century culture, mostly people in the entertainment world or sports figures. I was in Chicago once, changing planes just before that city's team, the Bears, was to play in the Super Bowl. You would not believe what I saw at the O'Hare Airport. The cult of Bear worshipers was in evidence everywhere. Bear memorabilia was on display in every shop. I was aware even then that, whether the Bears won or lost, they would be forgotten as new teams captured the spotlight. They are like all the idols created by public worship. They are worshiped only inasmuch as we buy tickets to their sports events or movies or concerts. Those idols are constantly changing, removed, and trampled, as new ones take their places.

Nature, that beautiful, often spectacular handiwork of God, is an idol for some. I feel grateful to live in the Pacific Northwest, where the grandeur and glory and beauty of nature are so evident. But, friends, make no mistake about it, nature is not our mother. That old mother-earth concept is pure paganism. Nature is the creation of the God revealed in the Old and New Testaments, the God incarnate in Jesus Christ. God is our Father, but nature is not our mother. Nevertheless, it is easy to slip into the worship of the beauty God has wrought and forget the Creator.

We can make an idol of someone we love, of course, a husband, wife or child, but even romantic fantasies can become an idol. A woman I know claims she has no love left for her husband. Presently, she has an overseas pen pal, someone she hasn't seen in years, but with whom she has been corresponding for a long time. "I could love that man so easily," she tells me. I suspect she loves the concept of romance, not that man. If he should come home and they were free to marry, I think her feelings might change. We can get very romantic about somebody we never see, maybe an old high school flame whose desirability has grown enormously in our imagination since we last saw him or her. Love is a commitment to the person God has given us—doing, saying, and being love to that person in good times and difficult times.

Even Christians can fall into the worship of idols. In subtle ways, some things other than God have become the object of our worship. It may be the church building. We are presently in the middle of a building program, and the idea of changing or tampering with our existing structure is to some almost sacrilegious. The sanctuary must remain as it is because they met the Lord there. The chapel cannot be changed because they were married there. Fortunately, for the most part, our congregation understands that it is not the event or experience we worship, but the Lord. But many of us fall into the trap of worshiping the holy place, of making pilgrimages from time to time, back to that little white chapel in our hometown, or that summer conference ground where God broke into our lives and consciousness for the first time.

Then there are the Christian gurus who seem to be idols to their followers. There are a good many around, from the solidly orthodox to the flamboyant and flakey. Even in the face of flagrant wrongdoing, we do not give up our idols easily.

We have outstanding music in our church, for which I rejoice, but I realize that the worship of music can sometimes undermine worship of God. There are those who can feel God's presence only in the great music of Bach, Beethoven, Handel, and the rest. Recently, we have begun to include praise songs in our services, and more than one person has commented along these lines: "At last, we're really worshiping."

I read not long ago that a friend wandered into Handel's room just as he was finishing the last notes of the "Hallelujah Chorus." He found the composer with tears streaming down his cheeks, the magnificent work completed on the desk in front of him. "I did think," Handel exclaimed to his friend, "I saw all heaven before me, and the great God Himself." Handel saw the living God, and his response was that famous, perhaps the most stirring hymn of praise ever written. We sing it, year after year, so faithfully and reverently. It is, in itself, almost an idol.

Then there is preaching. Have we made an idol of certain kinds of preaching? It's sound preaching only if we hear certain phrases often, such as "the blood of the Lamb," or "the Second Coming." It isn't sound preaching unless the preacher shouts a lot, waves the Bible, pounds the pulpit. It isn't sound preaching unless the preacher reads from the King James version of the Bible, or gives an altar call.

We can even make an idol of our particular order of worship. Some want precise and predictable liturgy. They want to know what's going to happen every Sunday. There are denominations where that is possible. You can go any place in the world and find the same service from the same prayer book without variation. There is merit in that, but not if it's the only framework in which God can speak to you.

Another part of the Christian church is just as hooked on innovation. If it has been done before, it is not of God. It has got to be fresh and new every Sunday. A while back, I read an account of a service at St. John the Divine, that great New York cathedral. At this Sunday afternoon mass, ten children on roller skates charged down the aisles during the Gloria. A Mesquite Indian fertility dance took place on the altar. The tuned gongs of a Balinese American gamelan, a group of Andean pipers and drummers, and a Latin pop band faced one another across the congregation, sometimes all playing at once, and the congregation sang along. Now that's innovation in the extreme. If you need all that going on in order to communicate with God, there is something wrong with your concept of God.

The great attraction of idols is that they are controllable, containable. But God is a moving, living God, who wants a relationship with you and me. He wants us on His road, moving down the highway of life—like Abraham and Sarah and all the rest of His faithful servants. When we are deflected into the worship of any one of the idols we have been talking about, we are saying, "I want a God that I can predict. A God I can keep in a box. A God who will always be in a certain place when I need Him." The living God is much more demanding. He's always out there ahead of us, and we've got to find His will and catch up with Him. That God is a jealous God. That is the message of the second commandment. He wants all of us, our lives, our love.

He is not insisting on perfection. In fact, there is evidence that He loved and honored more than a few scoundrels, such as King David. Their great redeeming quality is that they were crazy about God, devastated when they failed Him, desolate until they were restored to His good graces.

The kind of love God requires is not unlike the kind of love we want in human relationships. As we contemplate marriage, most of us are not looking for a perfect spouse who will never make a mistake. I think we are looking for somebody who, whatever other good qualities he or she has, delights in us, thinks we are terrific. God wants that relationship of love, dynamic and ever-fresh. We can start each day anew, asking to be His person, doing His will.

The second commandment speaks particularly about idols in the form of graven images, and let's examine a few familiar, modern-day graven images. There is a song that says, "I don't care if it rains or freezes, as long as I've got my plastic Jesus." There are a lot of folks driving around with a plastic Jesus on the dashboard. I wouldn't want to have to judge what that means. Is it an idol, protecting the driver from harm, taking the place of the living God? Or is it simply a reminder of Jesus and His love and protection?

A bronze serpent was used by Moses as a symbol of God's protection and healing presence. The book of Numbers, chapter twenty-one, tells about the Israelites being bitten by serpents in the wilderness, many of them fatally. Moses was directed to make a bronze snake and put it on a pole. Anyone bitten was to look at it, and he or she would be saved. The bronze serpent was a reminder that those who put their trust in God would be healed. About a hundred years later Hezzekiah became king of Israel, and the text tells us, "He did right in the eyes of the Lord." One of the things he did was to remove and destroy the idols which the Israelites seemed tempted to worship in every generation. The bronze serpent had again been raised, and people came to burn incense before it. Hezzekiah broke it into pieces, just as he had smashed the sacred stones, removed the high places and cut down the ashrau poles. Only the living God was to be worshiped.

There is much confusion about the crucifix, I think. It is intended to remind us of God's costly love for us in Jesus Christ. A good many Christians of all traditions, Roman Catholic, Greek Orthodox, and Protestant, use the crucifix as a reminder of a living, loving, redeeming God. But that symbol has for some become an object of worship. It is caressed, kissed, laid on the sick and endowed with magic properties.

I believe we are living in the age of the Spirit. Old Testament times represent the age of the Father, Creator. For a few brief years, just thirty-three to be exact, we lived in the age of the Son. Since His death and resurrection and the birth of the Church at Pentecost, we have been in the age of the Holy Spirit. Paul put it this way: "Christ in you, the hope of glory." In worshiping idols, we are trying to contain and control God. We can't do that. We are His creation, He is not ours. By our invitation, He is in us, alive in us.

To preach about that living God, week after week, year after year, is an awesome responsibility. In the midst of it all, most of us preachers are vulnerable to the subtle distractions and temptations which begin to undermine our own relationship with the living God. In the pressure to come up with something fresh, helpful, wise, relevant, scholarly, interesting, occasionally even dazzling, I, for one, sometimes fall short of the goal, which is that the Holy Spirit will use my efforts to make known God's love and will for all of us. To do anything less is to offer up graven images, a poor substitute for an experience of the living God.

11. What in God's Name?

One evening, a little girl was having bedtime prayers with her mother. She began by saying, "Dear Harold, please bless Mother and Daddy and all my friends." "Wait a minute," interrupted her mother, "who's Harold?" "That's God's name," was the answer. "God's name? Who told you that was God's name?" asked the puzzled mother. "I learned it in Sunday school, Mommy. 'Our Father, who art in heaven, Harold be thy name . . .'"

I feel certain God heard that little girl's prayers, even when He was called "Harold." But, exactly how important is it to know God's right name and call Him by that name? For that matter, how important is any name, yours or mine or anyone else's? Almost every name evokes an image, a personage behind the person, and that brings us to the third commandment. "You shall not misuse the name of the Lord, your God, for the Lord will not hold any guiltless who misuses His name." The more familiar translation is, "Thou shalt not take the name of the Lord thy God in vain." It is a commandment that seems unambiguous, and yet a lot of us have questions about what it means to misuse God's name, to take it in vain, and we are often more confused about how to rightly use God's name.

Ancient Israelites traditionally believed in the power in God's name, and rightly so. His name was never spoken lest they transgress on His majesty and glory. His name was not even written, except in symbols. The name derived from those symbols is Yahweh, or Jehovah, but that would never be written or spoken aloud.

In New Testament times, Jesus claimed there was power in His name. "Whatever you ask in my name, I will do it." It sounds like some kind of magic formula whereby we tack on "in Jesus' name" to insure that God will give us the desires of our hearts. Rather, we could liken it to coming into an audience with someone in the name of a president or a king. To come in Jesus' name is to come under His authority, carrying out His will inasmuch as we are able. In the name of Jesus, we have boldness to bring our petitions, to act, to work for the establishment of His Kingdom.

It is surprising how often in the biblical record God's blessings to His people come in the form of a new name. A man named Abram and his wife Sarah left their homeland in the urban Babylonian area and became nomads for God the rest of their lives. They owned no land until a burial tomb was required for Sarah, and the Cave of Macpelah was purchased. God's covenant with Abram was sealed with a new name—Abram is thought to mean "righteous father," while Abraham means "father of multitudes," which, of course, he became. The point is that God's covenant with His first faithful servant was sealed with the gift of a new name.

In subsequent generations, Abraham's grandson, Jacob, was given a new name. Jacob and his brother Esau were twins. Jacob was the secondborn, clutching his brother's heel at the moment of birth, seemingly contending with him even then for the birthright. That is the origin of his name, Jacob, which means "the supplanter" and which was to become synonymous with the quality of unsavory deception. He lived up to that name in the following years, cheating his brother and deceiving his father. That is the life he lived until that dark night of the soul when he wrestles with God by the brook Jabok. With a tenacity bordering on effrontery, he calls out, "I will not let you go unless you bless me." Does that offend you? Do you believe that God wants to bless you, wants you to demand your blessings, because blessing is His nature? Jacob's blessing was a new name. "Your name will no longer be Jacob ("supplanter, cheat") but Israel (which means "prince"). And that was the name for the nation to come through Jacob: Israel, a people who struggle with God and overcome.

Simon, the big fisherman, had traveled with Jesus and the twelve for a long time before he received his new name. In Matthew's gospel, the incident occurs in Ceasarea Philippi.

Jesus asks His disciples, "Who do the crowds say that I am?" They reply, "Some say John the Baptist, others say Elijah, and still others say that one of the prophets of long ago has come back to life." Their Master goes on to ask more pointedly, "But what about you? Who do you say that I am?" At this point, Peter makes his great statement of faith, "The Christ of God," meaning the predicted Deliverer, the Messiah for whom they had been waiting for centuries. Jesus responds, "Blessed are you, Simon, son of Jonah . . . and I tell you that you are Peter (Petros, Greek for "rock") and on this rock I will build my Church." The Church was built on Peter's confession of faith and that of all those to follow. Simon, the big, blustering fisherman, will be Peter, the spokesman for the apostles and the head of the church born at Pentecost.

One of my own New Testament heroes is Barnabas, a Levite from Cyprus, formerly called Joseph. He plays such a pivotal role in the early Church. He is one of the first to contribute financially to this new little faith community. He is a friend and companion of Paul, the brilliant apostle-preacher, the doctrinal architect of our faith. However, it is Barnabas who, on more than one occasion, smooths the way, diffuses hostility, makes peace between diverse factions. Early on, the apostles gave him his new name, which means, "son of encouragement." It is a name we might all aspire to. There is always a shortage of those people able to affirm and support, those who see God's hand and will in all situations, and who cheer and comfort the rest of us.

Our name conveys an identity, usually one given to us by our family. It's not always a positive identity. A lot depends on whether we felt loved and worthwhile in that setting from the earliest years on through adulthood. I have several Christian friends who have deliberately chosen a new and different name from the one they were given. They didn't like the messages conveyed by that name, or the person that name seemed to describe. A close friend who had used his middle name from boyhood recently changed his name to John, his original first name. He's making an effort to begin a new life with a new image, and, while it's hard for me to remember to call him John after all these years, I understand that it is important because it symbolizes a significant change in his life.

From time to time I counsel someone who grew up with an alcoholic parent, which almost always produces identity problems. Those children carry a great deal of guilt and shame about their mom or dad's addiction and usually shoulder far too much responsibility for the intolerable situation at home. I try to help them see that God offers a way out of that bondage. They need not remain that frightened, ashamed little girl or boy. They can have a fresh start in the household of faith, with new fathers, mothers, brothers, and sisters to help and encourage.

Sometimes we try to borrow an identity from the crowd we hang out with, or from particular people we admire and would like to be like. Most of us have had Christian role models along the way, and we find ourselves wanting to copy their style or personality. That is the dynamic at work in many successful youth programs. But, ultimately, any kind of spiritual impersonation is headed for failure, if not disaster. We think we can be like Rich Little, the famous impressionist. He can make us see and hear all sorts of well-known figures—Ronald Reagan, John Wayne, Richard Nixon, and many others. However, in a voice-scan test, it is immediately apparent that there is no similarity between Rich Little imitating President Reagan and the president's actual voice. A voice, yours or anyone else's, is noncounterfeitable, just like your fingerprints. Your spiritual identity is unique and unrepeatable, and the more you discover about that identity, the more you are what God intended you to be from the beginning.

Great things have been, and continue to be done in the power of God's name. The early disciples were in touch with that power to the extent that even Peter's shadow was thought to produce the healing of diseases. In the book of Acts, we find a magician named Simon watching the signs and wonders of the apostles and lusting after that kind of power for himself. He tries to buy the formula. What will it cost him to purchase that kind of power? Peter's rebuke is a stern one. "May your money perish with you because you thought you could buy the gift of God with money."

The real test of any name, I would say, is in the kind of feelings that name evokes. Let's say you're in a crowded room somewhere and someone calls out the name of someone you know who just entered the room. Perhaps it's someone you love. In my case, let's suppose it's my wife. Even after all these years, something in me delights in the fact that I'm going to see her, especially if it's unexpected. Her name evokes something magical because of our special relationship of love. I'm sure you can think of people like that, whose very names evoke in you some deep sense of joy and anticipation.

Which brings us to God's name and the feelings His name evokes. We have all been in situations where God's name is being used in vain, the very thing this third commandment addresses. God, Jesus, Christ—all names we Christians revere—are being used to punctuate conversation, sometimes in anger, but more often in the most casual way. I don't condemn whose who are doing that. I assume they don't know any better. They have no relationship of love with God or Jesus Christ, and their profanity is meaningless. But that doesn't keep me from cringing just a little and from wanting to protest, "Hey, friend, you're talking about someone I love."

I believe this third commandment has as much meaning for our lives today as it did in those ancient days when it was first given to the Israelites. First of all, it is a warning about being casual in the use of God's name. When we toss off a "by God" in the same way we would toss off a "by George," we are acting as if there is no God, or that He is so remote it doesn't matter. Someone by that name, in fact the Ultimate Being, is listening. He has warned us not to use His name lightly because in doing so we are making Him some far-off intellectual concept, instead of a living, loving Father with whom we are in relationship.

We are also warned about swearing in God's name. The old Jews took this seriously, and, as we said, were careful never even to use His name. The awesome God who spoke to Moses in the thunder and smoke of a mountain was not to be offended. They would instead swear by heaven, by earth, by the Temple, or by Jerusalem. Jesus warned them against doing even that. It is God who made heaven and earth, who made the Temple and Jerusalem. In swearing by those things, they were just one step away from swearing by the Creator. Jesus suggested that their word ought to be enough. "I will do it" or, "I will not do it." There is no need to emphasize those simple statements. Just state your intentions, and then carry them out.

Most of our swearing is idiotic, when you think about it. Let's say you hit your thumb with a hammer and make the usual response. God cannot damn a hammer—an inanimate object. It is an impossibility. It is an offense to assume that God would even consider that at your request. But, even more seriously, let's say somebody has offended you and, in anger, you ask God to damn that person. That is against His loving nature. We are damned and go to hell only by our own choice, not by God's. God's best will is that we all respond to His offer of love and eternal life. God does not damn anyone, and we offend Him if we suggest, ever so blithely that He will.

We are not to use God's name lightly and familiarly as if He is our servant, eager to do our bidding. Sometimes, in our arrogance about our knowledge of God or the length of our relationship with Him, we think we can manipulate Him. We begin to believe He is at our beck and call. We need to be careful that we do not attempt to make God our servant in our prayers. In his autobiography, W. C. Fields tells about a letter he received from a cousin in Ireland, and it is full of this attitude we are talking about. "Your cousin, Hughey Dougherty, was hung in Londonderry last Friday for killing a policeman. May God rest his soul, and may God's curse be upon Jimmie Roger, the informer. May his soul burn in Hell. The Protestants are terrible. They go through the country and shoot people down in the fields where they are working. God's curse on them . . ." The letter goes on in the same vein, and I doubt that it is genuine, but it is an extreme example of the dangerous use of God's name we are talking about. The whole idea that we can make use of Him to bless or to curse at our whim is more than foolish. It is offensive and arrogant. God is not our servant; we are His.

An oath taken in God's name is to be honored unequivocably. Your lawyers would certainly warn you about that if you were to testify in court. When you swear on the Bible to tell the truth and then perjure yourself, you are committing a crime, and a serious one. Any oath taken before God is not to be treated lightly. That is one of the reasons the Christian church has traditionally opposed divorce for those who were married in church or by a clergyman. Vows were taken before God and witnesses to love this partner in plenty and want, in sickness and health, until death do you part. How do you renege on that kind of vow and keep your integrity and self-esteem? Divorce is a common occurrence in our day, but I am aware of the toll it takes on the emotional well-being of those people of conscience who have been through it. A Christian friend remarked to me some years ago that "the dark night of the soul is always, the result of broken promises." They do come back to haunt us, as perhaps nothing else does.

If, then, we are not to take God's name in vain, how are we to use it? Most of us bring to that name certain preconceived expectations. Ideally, God's name ought to evoke in us love and faith. All the names of the Triune God—Father, God, Lord, Jesus, Christ, Holy Spirit—are names we call on in this dynamic relationship of love, and they can be used interchangeably in our prayers as we bring our concerns, intercede for others and listen for direction. But God's name is capable of evoking negative feelings as well—guilt and fear, for example. Does God want you to fail or succeed? Does He send healing or illness? Is He a God of law, or a God of grace and glory? Is God your Creator and Redeemer, on your side, caring for you?

My wife and I were worshiping with a friend in Florida some years ago when our friend heard a description of God that really startled her. We've known her for thirty years now, and in all those years she has been struggling with her relationship with her mother, who seems to have minimized and humiliated her from childhood on. It's been a constant struggle to reject the names her mother has given her—worthless, unlovely, and the rest—and claim her new identity as a child of God. This particular morning, it was Mother's Day, and the preacher was eulogizing mothers in general. His final sentence was this: "God's love is like a mother's love," with which our friend turned to us and whispered, "Oh, I hope not!"

Jesus is the ultimate revelation of God's nature and love. He says, "If you have seen me, you have seen the Father." In the face of Jesus, we see the God of the Old Testament, the God of the patriarchs and prophets, the God of creation. That is the God who loves you, who so loved the world that He gave His only Son for its redemption.

The book of Deuteronomy speaks of the *mezuzah*, a sign the Jews put over the door indicating they were God's people. I tell my congregation that I wish we could reintroduce that tradition. Imagine such a sign over the front door of every Christian's house, condominium, apartment, trailer, dormitory—whatever. "This place belongs to God, and may all that is done here be done in His name."

12. God's Labor Laws

The fourth commandment, which concerns the Sabbath, is among the most controversial of the Ten Commandments. Someone has said that our great-grandfathers referred to the seventh day as the Holy Sabbath, our grandfathers called it the Sabbath, and our parents simply said Sunday. Now, we speak about the weekend. True or not, we all would agree there has been a diminishment over the generations, and that the Sabbath is increasingly more secular and largely undistinguished from the other six days.

One of the best movies of recent years, *Chariots of Fire,* is unusual in that it is, in part, the story of a Christian, Eric Liddel, a famous runner who later became a missionary. Liddell, a traditional Scottish Christian, refused to run on Sunday, even in the Olympic Games and even when pressured by his government to do so. I am sure that was puzzling to most moviegoers—this concept of a God who requires such a strict observance of the Sabbath.

Perhaps your own childhood memories include that same strict observance of the Sabbath, of God's day of rest. I've met a good number of Presbyterians with those sorts of memories. Someone has said that being a Presbyterian doesn't keep you from sinning. It just takes all of the joy out of it. Some of my parishioners grew up in homes where the Sabbath was strictly observed. No work was to be done. Only the Bible was read, and no newspapers or books, not even religious ones. Games or recreation were out of the question.

My mother, as I've mentioned, was a devout Christian. My father was a deacon and a church officer, but really only a nominal Christian. He had a life-changing encounter with God the last year of his life, but prior to that church was not one of his priorities. Every Sunday, the issue of going to church was debated. About half the time, my mom won and we went. On the Sundays when we didn't go, I usually felt a little guilty. The demands of the Sabbath in my childhood were met simply by attending church. That hour of worship was a duty. Your obligations to God were fulfilled by being there.

One friend tells about growing up in a home of nonchurchgoers. She used to sneak out Sunday mornings to go to a Sunday school class in a nearby church. That illicit hour was the most love-oriented, creative part of her week. I love her story and the picture it paints of the church. The family of faith gathered on Sunday morning ought to be an irresistible attraction.

A good many of our new members, and we have over three hundred of those each year, were first brought to Church by their children. Those children, taken to Sunday school by friends and parents of friends, get hooked, and before long are evangelizing their parents. That Sunday school hour is changing their lives, and before long the entire family is remembering the Sabbath day, "to keep it holy."

In truth, though, this fourth commandment does not apply to Christians today, unless you are a Seventh Day Adventist. In the first eight hundred years of Christian history, believers did not keep the Sabbath, and had no intention of doing so. As a matter of fact, for some periods during those first eight hundred years, it was against church law to keep the Sabbath. It was considered a holdover from Judaism, as was circumcision, and such Judaizing was staunchly resisted. Ours was a new covenant in Christ, and those old rules no longer applied. Even the reformers, Calvin and Luther and the rest, did not stress observing the Sabbath.

But let's examine the heart and mind of God as we understand it to be revealed in this particular commandment. "Six days you shall labor and do all your work, but the seventh day is a Sabbath to the Lord your God." Jesus rose from the dead on the day after the Sabbath. The women who came to the tomb were not able to do so earlier because they were observing the

Sabbath, as all faithful Jews did. Henceforth, however, the first day of the week, the day when our Lord rose from the tomb, was observed as the holy day of the week, the day to honor and worship God. For almost two thousand years now, the first day of the week, honoring Jesus Christ the Lord, has been our "Lord's day." But that is a departure from the original Sabbath day described in the fourth commandment.

The very first description of Christian worship, apart from the biblical record, was written by Pliney, the governor of Bethynia. In the year 3, he was asked by his good friend, the Roman Emperor Trajan, to find out just what customs this strange new sect was practicing. Were those customs contrary to Roman law? Here is Pliney's reply:

> They were in the habit of meeting on a certain fixed day before it was light, when they sang in alternate verses a hymn to Christ as to a god, and bound themselves by a solemn oath not to commit any wicked deeds, but never to commit any fraud, theft or adultery nor deny a trust, when they should be called upon to deliver it up, after which it was their custom to separate and then reassemble to partake of food, but food of an ordinary and innocent kind [the agape feast, the Lord's Supper].

That, then, is how the Lord's day was observed in the second century. Believers gathered to honor Jesus, to sing hymns, to swear to live a pure and good life in charity to all and, finally, to partake of communion and go their way. Those are the roots of what continues to take place on Sunday morning in Christian churches all over the world.

It is helpful to remember the setting in which this fourth commandment was given. The Israelites were wandering in the wilderness, being fed on manna provided by God. They were instructed to gather manna only six days, and on that sixth day to gather enough for two days. The seventh day was to be a day of rest. This was a revolutionary idea. Prior to that time, everybody in the world worked seven days a week. There was no day of rest. People simply worked continually. Life consisted of total, unremitting labor.

The creation story provides a model, the pattern God wanted to set up for His creation. We read in Genesis that He created the world in six units of time and, on the seventh unit, he desisted from those labors and rested. We, being in His image, need that same rhythm of work and rest in order to be creative people, reflecting our Creator God. We can't work unceasingly. On the seventh day, labors are to stop. It is time to restore our minds and renew our bodies.

The word "sabbath" does not actually mean rest. The more accurate translation is "to desist." Keep in mind, too, that in those days there were very few "white-collar" jobs. Almost everybody worked physically—as shepherds, carpenters, plumbers, bakers, and in a host of other occupations. Apart from, perhaps, scribes or the members of a royal court, everybody did physical labor. In that context, we begin to appreciate God's loving concern for His people. On the seventh day they were to rest, by His command.

It was not a holy day in the sense that it was a day for worship. It was holy in its humanitarian thrust. To keep it holy, or set apart (which is what holy means) you were simply to desist from what you had been doing the rest of the week and, in most cases, that was grueling, physical labor. As I see it, the commandment reflects once again the relationship that God wants with His children. We are not animals. We are not slaves. We are made in God's image, and God rested. We are to do the same, to take a time in the week to recreate, to restore, to renew.

Many years ago, while I was doing graduate work at Boston University, we found housing out along the coast in a little community which was entirely Jewish. As far as I know, we were the only Gentiles there. It was a valuable lesson in how it feels to be a minority. On Saturday mornings, I'd be out in our little yard, playing with our two small kids. Our neighbors, on the other hand, were doing no work, observing the Sabbath, dressed in their best clothes. On the next day, as we put on our Sunday best and took off for Sunday school and church, they were out frolicking with their kids. I was struck, even at that time, with the powerful witness the Jews have been to the world over the centuries, especially in Old Testament times. They stopped their labors and desisted on the Sabbath day as no other people did. They were people keeping a covenant, following God's rules, as baffling as that must have seemed to the pagan societies all around them.

The theme of Exodus, as we have stated often, is that God is a delivering God, and the commandments are an important part of that deliverance. They are a blueprint for loving and serving God and living in charity and good will with our neighbors, and they reflect God's best will for His people. In this fourth commandment, God delivers us from meaninglessness. We were not born simply to pull burdens, to plow and sow and reap, to saw and drill and chop. We are made in the image of the Creator and work should have meaning. At its best, it is to be an expression of God's creative spirit. We are to be His people, in whom and through whom He thinks His thoughts and does His work and will in the world.

Martin Marty is without doubt our most prolific Christian writer today. He writes about four or five books a year and as many articles. I discovered just recently that Martin Marty loves to sit in a hot tub for two or three hours at a time and do a good part of his reading there. I was delighted to learn that, because it is something I love to do as well. It's a time to catch up on all the magazine and newspaper articles I've been saving to read. If Martin Marty does it, it must be OK. I'm going to quit feeling guilty about it. It is a practice in the spirit of the fourth commandment—to desist from the usual labors and to renew the spirit and restore the body.

I've been accused of having two speeds—full speed ahead and dead stop, and that's not all bad. If you cannot stop some of the time, relax your body and change your pace, you miss something of what God has planned for you. Work hard, rest completely, play enthusiastically, and worship wholeheartedly. That's the healthy rhythm God wants for your life and mine.

The fourth commandment is one means of delivering us from the tyranny of time. Time is a commodity we all have in limited amounts in this world. As it runs out, we start to get panicky. We dare not stop and do nothing. We forget that the Lord of time has advised us to do that periodically. Then there are the people whose lives are spent simply killing time, passing time in meaningless pursuits so that time itself is the oppressor. A poignant poem by a man named Raymond Carver puts it this way:

> I have a job with a tiny salary and an infinite eight-nine
> hours of work.
> I devour the time outside the office like a wild beast.
> Someday I hope to sit in a chair in another country,
> Looking out the window at fields of sugar cane or
> Mohammedan cemetaries.
> I don't complain about the work so much,
> As about the sluggishness of swampy time.
> The office hours cannot be divided up.
> I feel the pressure of the full eight or nine hours,
> Even in the last half hour of the day.
> It's like a train ride lasting day and night.
> In the end you're totally crushed.
> You no longer think about the straining of the engine,
> Or about the hills or flat countryside,
> But ascribe all that's happening to your watch alone.
> The watch that you continually hold in the palm of your hand,
> Then shake and bring slowly to your ear in disbelief.

It strikes a familiar chord, doesn't it? Do you remember that last period at school, waiting for freedom? This fourth commandment is God's reminder that we've got eternity. We need not panic. Let that one day of doing nothing remind you, as it did the Jews, that God is running the universe. You and your frantic efforts are not keeping it going.

We might ask what it means to keep the Lord's day, that day Christians have been celebrating for almost two thousand years. I believe it is to be marked, first of all, by joy. It was for the Jews in Old Testament times and to some degree it still is. The Psalmist urges us to "make a joyful noise unto the Lord." That will mean something different for each one of us. For you it may mean great choirs and orchestras, though most of us would not classify that as noise. The Jews made use of those and more. They had full orchestras, huge choirs, people shouting and dancing. They came into God's presence with hearts full of joy and praise.

There is a Roman church in Philadelphia called the Church of the Most Precious Blood of Jesus, which in recent years has been making a joyful noise unto the Lord. It was a totally white congregation until the late fifties and sixties, when the middle class moved to the suburbs. It became increasingly a black congregation, but soon that membership began to decline seriously. The turnabout occurred when the priest realized that many of his parishioners were going home after mass to listen to gospel music, and he started to structure the service in that direction. They have begun to celebrate in wild and wonderful ways. A fifty-voice syncopated choir comes down the aisle to start the service shouting, "Wake up and give Him honor!" People are free to shout throughout the service. When the mass gets dull, someone may call out, "Thank you! Hallelujah!" This Roman Catholic congregation comes singing, dancing, praising, and shouting into God's presence. We aren't that free in our congregation, but we are being delivered more and more from gloom and joylessness. In our Calvinistic way, we are trying to make a joyful noise unto the Lord.

Ben Weir, the Presbyterian missionary who was for so long a hostage in Lebanon, speaks movingly about worshiping while in captivity. Every Saturday night, he saved a piece of bread from dinner, and on Sunday morning he would eat that piece of bread and feel so moved by the sense of communing with God's people all over the world. Even in prison, he found a way to celebrate being in the presence of the Lord.

The Sabbath was designed, as we said, for those who worked hard physically the other six days. Some of us still do physical labor, of course, but more and more of us, I suspect, sit behind desks all week long and need some physical exercise. Fortunately, in our country, we have only a five-day work week with two free days. We have a Saturday in which to change pace, to rest or exercise, depending on our needs. If you sit all week long, physical work is refreshing. But, in desisting from what we regularly do, we are fulfilling God's plan for us as we see it laid forth in the fourth commandment.

A pastor friend had open heart surgery some months ago. The doctors replaced a valve in his heart, and he shared some of what is happening to him as a result of that experience. "I no longer feel guilty about playing golf. God told me to be a steward of my body, and I sit around too much. When I play golf or ski or anything like that, it's a way of honoring God."

We have been talking about "God's labor laws," and as they are set forth in this fourth commandment they are certainly simple enough. But, as most of us know, they were corrupted by the legalists. Even Jesus was accused of not keeping the Sabbath as it was interpreted by the legalists. But Jesus understood well that the Sabbath was God's good gift to renew and restore His people, and that they ought to come into His presence rejoicing. Jesus reminded them that the Sabbath was made for people, people were not made for the Sabbath. Those legalists served a God who had so many rules about keeping the Sabbath that it was almost impossible to fulfill all the requirements and, in that event, God would smash them. The tragedy is that they missed entirely the intent of God's law concerning the Sabbath.

The legalizers turned this fourth commandment into a hopeless maze of what was and was not permitted. Volumes were written, for instance, defining work. Can a man pick up a stone on the Sabbath? No, he can't. Can a father pick up his son? Yes, that's not a burden. But, should the son have a stone in his hand, picking him up would be work, depending on the size of the stone. You see the problem with legalism. There is never an end to it. All the blessings God intended by means of the Sabbath were lost in the endless nitpicking over the rules.

The Puritans in Britain were strict Lord's day people. There was little joy or celebration in their worship. The Scots were perhaps the most guilty of the legalism we're talking about. My wife's grandmother, a staunch Church of Scotland Aberdonian, cooked all Sunday's food on Saturday. No work was done and no frivolity of any kind was tolerated on Sunday. For a time, no trains ran in Scotland on Sunday. Everything came to a standstill. In 1872, a Sunday run between Edinburgh and London was initiated, and the reaction was predictably violent.

Church people and their pastors came en masse to picket the railroad station. Would-be travelers were told, "You're buying a ticket to Hell if you get on that train." They entirely missed the meaning of either the Sabbath or the Lord's day, though, as we said, they are not the same. Nevertheless, both are gifts, one to restore and refresh and one to come into God's presence with joy and thanksgiving. As I hear about Sunday at my wife's grandmother's house, it was neither refreshing nor joyful.

As for present-day Christians in our own nation, there are no set rules about observing the Lord's day except, of course, for worship. The rest of the day may be for you a family day, a day for study or recreation. But whatever we're doing, we need to be aware that our non-Christian neighbors are observing us as pagan societies watched the old Jews. What we do and do not do is a powerful, though silent witness. Whatever else we do on that day, may our sense of joy and celebration be contagious. Let's remember the Lord's day and keep it holy.

13. Honoring Mom and Dad

Jesus, when asked about the Ten Commandments, summed them all up in just two. "Love the Lord your God with all your heart, mind, and strength and your neighbor as yourself." Up to now, we've been talking about loving God in the manner He has prescribed. He insists on being the only god in our lives, and we must put no idols or graven images in place of Him. His name is not to be misused, and we are to set apart one day a week to rest and to honor Him. Beginning with the fifth commandment, however, we move into the second emphasis—loving our neighbor as ourself. These next six commandments deal with our social and civil obligations. They provide the guidelines for living peacefully and lovingly with each other, and they form the basis for a just and godly society.

The first of those civil and social commandments, the fifth commandment, is the only one that promises a reward. "Honor your father and your mother, so that you may live long in the land the Lord your God is giving you." It seems rather a mild injunction compared to the later ones against murder, stealing, adultery, and the rest, but for the old Jews, that commandment was of primary importance. Perhaps it is not accidental that it is the first issue dealt with in regard to our social responsibilities. The old "charity begins at home" maxim might apply here. As we deal honorably and lovingly with our parents, we learn to apply that same charitable behavior to the rest of God's family.

We find this commandment reinforced throughout the Old and New Testaments. In Leviticus 20 and Exodus 21, we read that, "If anyone curses his father or his mother he must be put to death." Leviticus adds, "and his blood is on his own head." In Proverbs 20:20 we read, "If a man curses his father or mother, his lamp will be snuffed out in pitch darkness." The penalties for disobeying this fifth commandment were grim and graphic.

In the fifteenth chapter of Matthew's gospel and the seventh in Mark's, Jesus talks about the custom called *corban*. The Jews were morally and religiously obligated to care for their parents, particularly as they grew older and were less able to care for themselves. But they had invented very clever ways of avoiding those obligations. One was by telling their parents that the money they would have gained is now *corban*, meaning "given to God." Since it was God's, you could avoid using it to support your parents. Jesus took them to task for this duplicity and for their selfish disregard of the needs of their parents. Harsh words were spoken to those Jews who had found a legal loophole to avoid caring for their parents.

We know Jesus took the fifth commandment seriously, because of a later incident. His mother, Mary, is thought to have lost her husband, Joseph, when Jesus was still very young. For most of his adult life, Jesus stayed home in Nazareth, his hometown, and worked in the carpenter shop, and we assume he supported his mother. In those last hours on the cross—the most horrible death anyone could ever experience—His last thoughts were about His mother. Seeing her grief and distress and in concern for her future, he puts her in the care of the beloved disciple, John. He said to her, "'Dear woman, here is your son,' and to the disciple, 'Here is your mother.' From that time on, this disciple took her into his home" (John 19:26–27).

In the biblical record, the family has been the keystone of society since Genesis and the first family, Adam and Eve, Cain and Abel. God put His children in families, and that unit is largely the fabric that holds society together. There was an attempt early on in Communist Russia to change that. They tried to abolish the family as a unit and to replace family loyalty with government loyalty. It was an unsuccessful effort.

This fifth commandment was, I think, my mother's favorite. I never heard her say much about the others. She never lectured against lying or stealing or commiting adultery. But she talked to me often about honoring your mother and father. One of her recurring lines was, "Son, I hope that someday you have a son just like you and that he treats you just the way you're treating me." I probably deserved that remark and, sad to say, as I got older and understood her better and tried to be more loving, I never heard that line any more. I'd like to turn the meaning of that statement around, though, for my own two sons and my daughter, who are now all adults. I hope their children treat them exactly the same way they are treating their mother and me, which is with love and respect and even appreciation. I could wish no more for them than that.

Then there was my dad. He too had some not-so-subtle ways of reinforcing this commandment. One of his favorite stories was Grimm's fairy tale about the little boy who lived with his parents and an old grandfather. The little boy and the old man were great pals, but, as the grandfather got older, the parents grew more and more contemptuous of him. He dribbled and spilled at the table to the extent that his son built him a trough-like plate, and he was required to eat in the corner alone. One day the little boy's father finds him in the basement building something and asks what it is. The lad replies, "I'm building a trough for the day when you get old, daddy." I probably heard that story from my dad fifty times in my growing-up years. I think he was trying to tell me something.

As I think about those two stories, I'm aware that my parents must have had a deep fear of not being honored as they grew older. I think now that fear had less to do with me than it did with their guilt feelings and unfulfilled relationships with their own parents. My mother's mother died young, and her father remarried and fathered eleven other children. He sent her to America as an unwilling immigrant at age thirteen. My father left Sweden and his mother and father and sister at age twenty-one and never saw any of them again. Both of my parents must have wanted to insure that I would obey this commandment in ways that they had been unable or unwilling to do.

As we said, a promise comes with this commandment—that your days may be long in the land. Actually, that could be construed as either a threat or a promise. If we do not honor our parents, will God rub us out with a coronary at an early age? I don't think so. That's not the nature of the God revealed in the Bible or the God of our own experience. He does not threaten us. But the Giver and Creator of life knows how it works even more than do all our *present-day* psychiatrists and analysts, from Freud on. Most of those therapists understand that growth and well-being are often tied into forgiving and honoring our parents. If we can release all those negative feelings, life is more likely to be long and prosperous. Psychological health requires making peace with our parents, whether they deserve it or not.

I think, though, that we need to sort out what it means to honor our parents. Sometimes Satan, the father of lies, tries to distort the meaning and create in us a lot of false guilt. We think, for example, that to honor our parents we must obey them. That interpretation applies only to children and not to adults. In the sixth chapter of Ephesians, we read, "Children, obey your parents." But as we move into adulthood and maturity, the relationship is no longer that of rule-giver and rule-follower. Jesus honored His mother, as we said. But on the occasion where she came to a meeting where He was teaching and tried to interfere and take Him home, He did not obey her. He was not under her authority, but that of His heavenly Father. Further, he said that those who did the Father's will were his mothers and brothers as much as those blood relatives.

The second distortion of this commandment in regard to our parents is that we have to like them. You can love anyone you choose to, even your enemies. But you need not like everyone. Liking presupposes enjoying, and that's a spontaneous emotion we have no control over. You may like your parents or you may not, but honoring them has nothing to do with that. You may always want to take your father along on a fishing trip. You may want to ask your mother to play tennis or come for the weekend. But if that's not enjoyable, you are not required to build your life around them. We fall into the trap of thinking that unless our parents are our best friends, we are failing as sons or daughters.

Honoring your parents requires at the least that we do not shame them. Any child growing up in any home with one or two parents has material at hand to shame those people. We've caught them in those off moments when they have been dishonest, nasty, mean, small, and we are in a position to use that ammunition against them, with the rest of the world. We are not to do that. Those *Mommy Dearest* type books, whether they are true or false, are cheap shots. We could all write a similar book, similar in spirit, at least, hopefully without those lurid details. Fortunately, most of us don't have the skills or the service of a ghostwriter to do that.

But we can shame our parents verbally with those willing to listen. "What do you think my mother has done now? Have you heard how my father humiliated me when I was ten?" I'm not suggesting, by any means, that children of any age ought not to speak out about genuine abuse—physical, sexual, or emotional. I'm talking here about minimizing and humiliating those people who have invested years in us. We need not share their feet of clay with the world.

Noah's three sons had an opportunity to shame him. Most of us associate Noah solely with the building of the ark. When the ark finally landed, however, Noah planted a vineyard. When the grapes were ripe he made wine and got drunk and fell down naked in his cave. Shem, one of his three sons, discovered him in that state and went tattling to the other two. Their response was admirable. They got a garment, walked into the cave backward, and covered him, their faces turned to avoid seeing their father's shame. When they could have clucked and criticized, they honored him.

The second trap we can fall into with our parents is to idolize them. They are not God. They are not even little gods. They are just little children like you who grew up and got old. Those wrinkles are not a sign of superior wisdom. As we get older, we are usually surprised to find that our parents weren't really all that wise. When we have idolized our parents, it's hard to forgive them any failures or shortcomings. We believe they should have known better, or behaved more circumspectly. Whatever your parents were or weren't, believe they did the best they knew how and that they probably aren't and weren't much wiser than you.

One of my favorite comics is entitled "For Better or for Worse" and it's about family life, a mother and dad and two kids. In a recent episode, the first three segments show the mother tossing and turning in her bed, worrying about her ten-year-old son, Michael. She says, "Are we too tough on Michael? Are we not tough enough? Do we give in too often? Too seldom? Do we listen? Do we understand? Maybe I nag too much. Am I a good parent? Where are the answers? How does one know what to do?" In the last box we see Michael lying awake in his bed saying, "Trouble with grown-ups is they think they know everything."

It seems easy to feel cheated in the parent department, but we are discovering more and more that even the best parents, the most loving and wise, are not always able to be what they need to be in difficult situations. A study was begun a year or more ago at George Washington University by Dr. David Reece on patients undergoing dialysis treatment for kidney failure. They were trying to find out what kind of home environment promotes healing during this radical procedure. They anticipated that loving, supportive, intimate families would best aid the healing process. They found just the opposite. People on dialysis without warm, intimate families seemed to fare better.

One explanation for that finding is that a life-threatening illness within a close family is so frightening to other members, that the family closes the sick person out, even begins to expel him or her prematurely. They cannot handle the prospect of grief and loss. The uncaring family, on the other hand, simply bears it all stoically, even philosophically, as the family member goes through treatment. Whatever that study indicates, the point is that your destiny and well-being does not hinge totally on the kind of parents you had or have, wise or unwise, good or bad.

Certainly there are some obvious dimensions of honoring our parents that we need to mention. We are to be kind to our parents. We are to respect them. We are to care for them emotionally and, if necessary, financially. Most of all, we need to forgive our parents. If we do that, we will live long in the land which the Lord our God gives us. Gratitude is an important part of honoring our parents. Whatever they were, positive or negative, they have given you the gift of life.

We honor them by acting in their best interest, not ours. I talked to a friend whose mother is dying. "She's very old and frail," explained my friend. "I had to tell the doctors she wanted no 'heroic measures.' You can't imagine how guilty I felt." "But you did the thing that she would want, not the thing that makes you feel good," I assured her. "You honored her by letting her die peacefully with dignity, as she hoped to do." My friend's dilemma is a familiar one these days. We cannot bear the pain of parting with this beloved person. Therefore, we insist on prolonging his or her life far beyond the point where that life is bearable, let alone meaningful.

A young man recently told me the story of his remarkable mother. "I was a young boy of twelve with three younger brothers and sisters when my father died of a heart attack at age forty-two. My mother told me to never try to take my father's place. 'Don't try to be your daddy; just be my son.' She accepted the role of father and mother to all of us as teenagers. She went back to work for very little wages as a secretary in the sixties. Basically, she raised us all by herself with no welfare, no food stamps. When we were all grown up and out of the house, she took a job as one of the first group-home managers with six mentally retarded children. She had the same group for ten years and literally raised them all from the age of six . . . I love and honor my mother for having raised us in our rebellious years. I respect her more than anyone else in the world." That courageous mother obviously deserves honor; but, whoever your parents are or were, they were instruments of God to bring you life. Honor them for that.

I read not long ago about a practice of Henry Kissinger's when he was our nation's Secretary of State. Every time an aide brought him a report he would scowl and say, "Is that the best you can do?" He made that remark even before he read the paper. The answer was always "No," and the paper was then rewritten and invariably improved. That tactic apparently produced excellence. Many of us had parents like that. We could never satisfy them. Our marks were not high enough, and our achievements fell short of their expectations.

Someone has said that the older a father gets, the farther he had to walk to school. It's the classic guilt-producing story. "When I was your age, son, let me tell you how hard life was." My father was fond of telling me how much he idolized his father. "I would sit at his feet," he would say, "and wonder what I could do right now to please him." That was scarcely the way I related to my father, and the comparison always made me feel ashamed.

Finally, all parents leave a legacy to their children, whether they intend to or not. Two members of our congregation went off to the city of Nazareth a few years ago as missionaries, to live and work with Arab Christians there. They came back with many wonderful stories, but one concerned a man named Abu Hacham. His was part of a very wealthy Palestinian family back in the sixties before the Six-Day War. They owned one thousand acres on the West Bank. During the war, the Israeli army moved them out with the promise that they would be returned when the war ended. That was twenty years ago and they still have not been moved back. Presently, the Israelis are trying to buy this land from Hacham for five cents on the dollar. He refuses to sell. "I have titles. My family has owned that land for hundreds of years." Meantime, the Israelis possess the land and he doesn't. They tell him he has no choice but to sell.

Hearing that tale, the two visitors asked, "Aren't you bitter?" "Oh, no," he explained, "If I'm bitter, they've won. I have a son and some day, whether I pass on the land or not, I want to pass on to him the legacy of hope, not the legacy of bitterness." Abu Hacham is planning a legacy for his son even more valuable than that West Bank acreage. We are all, as parents, passing on a legacy of one kind or another. The Bible says, "The parents have eaten sour grapes and the children's teeth are set on edge." Let's say someone has hurt us—mother, father, friend, business partner—and we become bitter. Our kids are raised by that angry, disillusioned parent and they become bitter.

Don't let that happen to you. Leave a legacy of hope, of joy, of love. Honor your father and mother—as we said, not for their sakes but for yours—that your days may be long in the land which the Lord your God gives you.

14. A Matter of Life and Death

Of all the commandments, the sixth commandment, you shall not kill—or, more accurately, you shall not murder—is perhaps the most universally honored by both Christians and non-Christians. Above all, it reveals to any and all, whatever their faith or lack of it, who God is. He is a loving Father. He cares for each of His children equally. Human life is precious because it is His gift. The sixth commandment conveys a reverence for life that presupposes a loving Creator and His concern for and involvement with His creation.

The value of human life is the issue behind so many of the concerns discussed on the front pages of our newspapers, on television news, in magazines. We read the pros and cons of all these issues almost daily—nuclear arms, war, abortion, euthanasia, living wills, the death penalty, gun control, withdrawal of life-support systems from the terminally ill. At stake in all these issues is the value of human life, and looming dramatically in the background is God's simple and clear directive, "Thou shalt not kill."

There are, of course, societies in which life is cheap. Terrorism is acceptable. Innocent people, often school children, are killed for political reasons. The world calls those societies degenerate. The Nazis, to the extent that they killed six million people for political reasons, were degenerate. There are societies where children are routinely and callously murdered. In China, for example, we are told that female infants are frequently disposed of. They are considered an unprofitable and unnecessary burden to poor parents. Samuel Pulei, the first Masai pastor in the Presbyterian Church of East Africa and a personal friend, tells of being abandoned to die as a baby. He was very sickly and a hindrance to his tribe's nomadic life, and so he was left outside the compound at night for the lions and leopards to dispose of. The miracle is that the wild animals did not eat Samuel that night. His survival was a sign to his mother that he would live. God had great plans for Samuel and his life was miraculously spared.

What is the worth of a single life? Thirty pieces of silver? Three million pieces of silver? A human life is without price, of course. It is the most precious gift in the world. I occasionally like to remind my congregation assembled for worship that they are, each one, surrounded by priceless creations on both sides, in front and behind. Each person is the product of countless generations in a long line reaching back to Adam and Eve. Even in this age of test-tube babies, not one of us can be replicated or identically cloned. We are one of a kind works of art—genetically speaking, each one is a Rembrandt.

Let's examine, first of all, how the Old Testament Jews interpreted this commandment. As I indicated, the word in the original language is not "kill," but "murder," which is an important distinction. All the later translations reflect this more accurate version of the commandment. Thou shalt not murder. The difference is obvious. Killing is usually a spur-of-the-moment reflex action, in some cases, self-defense or accidental. Murder is premeditated, planned, violent, and unauthorized killing. In the first recorded murder, Cain slew his brother, Abel. His actions were the result of a long-term hatred and envy of his brother.

Interestingly, in Old Testament times this commandment did not apply to execution. Execution was practiced without compunction. Traditionally, there were four forms of execution. First was stoning, and it was not the kind we read about in the New Testament stoning of the martyr Stephen. The offender was put down a well and boulders were dropped on him or her. The offended party had the privilege of dropping the first boulder. If that didn't do the job, a second boulder was dropped, or a third, or however many were required to crush and kill the wrongdoer. In execution by stoning, death was not left to chance.

Then there was execution by burning. A man or woman was buried up to the neck in a pit. The mouth was forced open and hot lead was poured into it. It was said to be a quick and merciful death, though there were no survivors to attest to that. Offenders were also executed by beheading and strangulation, both of which (if you concede death by hanging is strangulation) have been practiced throughout history.

Execution was the penalty for nine different crimes: (1) murder as defined by the sixth commandment; (2) child-sacrifice; (3) manslaughter—unpremeditated killing; (4) keeping an ox known to be dangerous, if the ox eventually kills someone (you could liken that crime to the pitbull incidents of today); (5) bearing false witness on a capital charge; (6) kidnapping; (7) insult or injury to parents (penalty was death by stoning); (8) various forms of sexual immorality: incest, unchastity, adultery and unnatural vice, fornication by a priest's daughter or by someone betrothed; and (9) various religious ritual offenses such as: witchcraft and magic, idolatry, blasphemy, false claims of being a prophet, intrusion into sacred places, and Sabbath-breaking.

With all of this detailed planning for methods of execution for nine separate offenses, a Sanhedrin—the local ruling body of Pharisees—that executed more than one person every seven years was called a murderous Sanhedrin. In spite of the broad license for capital punishment, it was unusual to have an execution more than once every seven years. That is surprising and can only be explained by the great reverence for life the Israelites felt.

There were also, in those times, six cities of refuge for those accused of unpremeditated murder. Those sanctuary cities were located within a day's travel from any place in Palestine. You were safe there from the angry relatives of the victim, who might be bent on revenge. The sanctuary city is one more indication of the many provisions to protect life.

In the New Testament, Jesus speaks specifically to this commandment, "Thou shalt not murder." He begins by saying He has come to fulfill the law, and then goes on to deal with this commandment.

> You have heard that it was said to the people long ago, 'Do not murder, and anyone who murders will be subject to judgment.' But I tell you that anyone who is angry with his brother will be subject to judgment. Again, anyone who says to his brother, 'Raca,' is answerable to the Sanhedrin. But anyone who says, 'You fool!' will be in danger of the fire of hell. Therefore, if you are offering your gift at the altar and there remember that your brother has something against you, leave your gift there in front of the altar. First go and be reconciled to your brother; then come and offer your gift. (Matthew 5:21–24)

Jesus' hearers must have been as stunned as we are by His all-encompassing definition of murder. For by it, we are suddenly all guilty. Our lack of love is murder. Our anger is murder. Our idle insults are murder. Our unwillingness to be reconciled to our brother is murder. At the stoning of Stephen, Paul stood by consenting to his death; in later years, in his converted state, he was haunted by his role in that murder. Murder is more than taking our brother's life physically. We take that life by all sorts of subtle means—gossip, lies, unjust laws, economic exploitation, oppression, persecution, even uninvolvement. The list is endless.

In the name of sport, we deliberately set out to harm our brother. Boxing is the example that comes to mind most readily. Prize-fighting fans love to watch two men try to injure and maim each other. Even football, and I'm a football addict, is questionable in the light of this broad interpretation of the sixth commandment. In some cases, the game is preceded by a locker-room prayer, after which those men head out to crush their opponents as ferociously as possible.

As we indicated, this particular commandment is and was the most universally accepted, not just by the Jews, but by almost every culture since. In 1485, there was a turning point in English history at Bosworth in a battle between King Richard

III, the soon-to-be-King, and Henry VII. Richard was a true Englishman. Henry was more Welsh and French than English and had hardly ever been in England. Richard was a great soldier. Henry was not. Richard had twice as many men. Richard's army had the high ground. Henry was foundering in the swamps. Nevertheless, in two hours Richard was defeated. Henry became the first Tudor king of England, and no king since has been named Richard. Historians explain it this way. The word was out that Richard had had his two little nephews murdered in the Tower of London. Disgusted by this cold-blooded act, half of his army refused to fight for him and instead stood on their arms on Ambien Hill. The rumor, though still unproven, that Richard had taken two innocent little lives cost him the throne.

The pacifist interpretation of this commandment is that killing is never justified under any circumstances. I have had many discussions about this, mostly with Mennonite friends. I pose the usual hypothetical questions: "What if you came upon somebody attacking your wife and children, intending to kill them?" "What about the police? Shouldn't they be able to carry guns and be licensed to kill in extreme situations?" "What about a justifiable war with a noble goal which, as a nation, we considered the second World War to be?" "What about self-defense?" "What if somebody crashed into one of your worship services with an automatic machine gun and began to open fire indescriminately? Assuming you had a weapon available, would you not be justified in killing that person?" My friends answer all those questions with the same unwavering recital of the sixth commandment. "Thou shalt not kill."

That is not where I am, as you might have guessed. Without doubt, love is the number one virtue. But love and discipline go together and that discipline, in some cases, may have to take extreme forms. Our church's session has spent time recently trying to come up with a policy covering the discipline of off-base or wayward members. Our love for the brethren has limits in the sense that unrepentant behavior that is contrary to God's laws is unacceptable. If that is true on such a small scale within a close fellowship of believers, how much more necessary is this kind of discipline in our fragmented, difficult-to-monitor society? In some cases, I believe taking a life is the only possible course if we are to serve and protect the rest of society. God's law seems to make adequate provision for this view.

There seem to be two dangers in regard to this sixth commandment. One is to dismiss it because, as defined by Jesus, we are all murderers. The other is to assume that we keep it. If you are in the latter group, I worry about you. If you've never hated anybody, you're not alive.

A new member of our church came to see me recently. He told me bluntly he wanted to check me out. He had read a book devoted to attacks on various well-known Christians, including me. He told me he had since bought one of my books and found I was considerably more orthodox than he had been led to believe. Later on, though, I reflected on the interesting fact that he had bought the "anti" book first. Only after reading all the "antis" did he attempt to learn if there were any "pros" in regard to my theology. Then I recognized that as a familiar pattern, something I have done as well. There is something perverse in me that wants to read the scandal sheet. I want to read the exposés, the charges and suspicions. That's far more interesting than goodness, morality and orthodoxy.

A scene in Dostoyeveski's book *The Brothers Karamazov*, provides an interesting insight. An angry, vengeful man is asked at one point why he hates a particular person so much. He replies, "He had done me no harm. But once I played him a dirty trick, and I have hated him ever since." I think Dostoyevski hit on a strange truth. The people I hate are the people I have failed and betrayed, and to salve my own guilty feelings, I begin to find reasons to resent them.

But hatred is just one form of murder, and you can be free of that emotion entirely and still break the sixth commandment, with nothing stronger than deprecatory comments. Anything short of love for our brother, even the murderer, jeopardizes our very soul. Apart from the Savior, there is no hope for us. The apostle Paul writes, "Who will rescue us from this body of death? Thanks be to God—through Jesus Christ our Lord!"

15. "Whom God Hath Joined . . ."

In the years I have been in the pastorate, I have performed many weddings. I confess to you that I usually cry at most of them just a little. Those are tears of joy, I hasten to add. I've gotten to know these two people in counseling, and I am aware that they are on the threshold of a great adventure. In the days and years ahead, a synergy will take place whereby the two will become more than the sum of their separate parts. God's plan for marriage is that these two will be one flesh, a new creation.

Part of that plan includes sexual oneness. God is the author of romance, and sex is His powerful and mysterious gift. We are in a time, however, when sex has lost its mystery. It is used to sell every conceivable product, not just perfume and cosmetics but cars, refrigerators, drinks, both soft and hard, blue jeans, and breakfast cereal. It wouldn't surprise me if stocks and bonds were next. In light of our present-day attitudes, the seventh commandment, "Thou shalt not commit adultery," must seem to some like a quaint vestige of another time. But for many in the household of faith, this commandment is second only perhaps to murder in the hierarchy of God's laws.

I am sure it is the least popular of God's commandments. But, as with the rest of God's word, we are not free to choose only our favorite parts—at least not if we are serious about our faith. As we examine all of the ramifications for our lives today, let's remember that all ten commandments are the gift of a loving God, including the seventh. As we have said, He is the harbormaster who provides us with channel markers that the vessel of your life and mine might sail safely through the perilous reefs and rocks into the harbor.

Love, sex, and marriage are all parts of God's good gifts to His children. We sometimes get the impression, however, that the Hugh Hefners or Larry Flynts of the world invented sex. They simply capitalize on our God-given appetites and feed those appetites in distorted, even perverted ways. I've always felt somehow pleased that Jesus' first miracle was performed at a wedding service. Friends were being married in Cana and He was one of the guests, there to celebrate and rejoice. At His mother's request, He turned water into wine when the host's supplies ran out. He made sure the festivities could continue. In the tradition of the Jews, marriage is a sacred and inviolate covenant, and Jesus was a participant in witnessing that covenant on that occasion.

C. S. Lewis said, "We grow up surrounded by propaganda in favor of unchastity." What a trick the forces of evil have played upon us! They have made us believe that the real fun is in unlicensed, unbridled promiscuity. God, on the other hand, must be some kind of Victorian prude. The Victorian era was characterized by its denial of sexuality and by a good bit of hypocrisy. I heard about two very prim ladies of that era who were sitting on the porch one morning watching a bunch of chickens scratch around in the yard. A rooster suddenly appeared and began to chase one of the hens. In her attempts to escape, she ran out on the road and was hit by a carriage. "You see, Elsie," confided one of the ladies to her friend, "she'd rather die."

The Christian view of sex should be anything but Victorian. Sex is not some nasty, naughty practice that spiritual people don't engage in or, if they do, only for procreation. Sex, for the Christian, is that mysterious God-given means by which "these two shall be one." One of my favorite authors is Miguel Cervantes, the author of *Don Quixote*. It is a story familiar to almost everyone, thanks to the success of the musical *The Man of La Mancha*. It concerns a crazy old nobleman who sees the best in everyone. At the end Quixote says, "Too much sanity may be madness, but maddest of all is to see life as it is and not as it should be." Too often we see life as it is, not as it should be, and we settle for cheap and sleazy versions of love. We trade integrity and loyalty and sometimes our very soul for the transitory excitement of some illicit, shabby liaison. That is what adultery is all about.

This seventh commandment does not refer to fornication or premarital sex or homosexuality. Adultery is a sexual relationship which flouts the marriage vows. Whether you are the married partner or the third party cohabiting with the wife or husband, this is the sin the seventh commandment condemns. Let's examine now some of the reasons for this clear, unequivocable command, and why it is in our own best interests to take it seriously.

First of all, in the amazing gift of marriage, two people really do become one organism, one creation. "Whom God has joined together let no man put asunder." Monogamy is very much like monotheism. The first commandment requires us to forsake all the lesser gods of other faiths and religions, of other philosophies. Instead, we put all our chips on the fact that there is one Creator God whose name is Jesus. We bet our lives on Him. We are to do that same thing in marriage. We are to commit ourselves to our partner for better or for worse, for richer or for poorer, in sickness and in health. To hurt that partner is to wound ourselves. One man has said, "Deceiving my wife is like trying to sneak a sunrise past a rooster." To cheat on one's spouse is to chop that living organism into pieces and to leave it wounded, often mortally.

Adultery is not only a sin against your partner, it is a sin against God. When two Christians marry, or two Jews for that matter, they are making a covenant with God and each other. The relationship is triangular and three-dimensional. After Joseph was sold into slavery by his brothers, he served in the household of a wealthy Egyptian named Potiphar. When his master's wife tried to seduce him, Joseph refused her with these words: "How can I do this great wickedness and sin against God?" It was not just a matter of betraying his master who trusted him. Adultery would be a sin against God. In 2 Samuel, the prophet Nathan pointed out to King David that he had committed a horrible crime. David had Uriah, a lieutenant in his army, killed, because he coveted Uriah's wife, Bathsheba. In response, David said to Nathan, "I have sinned against the Lord."

God cares about our morality, our chastity, our purity. He says in Jeremiah 5, "Why should I forgive you? Your children have forsaken me and have sworn by gods that are not gods. I supplied all their needs, yet they committed adultery and thronged to the houses of prostitutes. They are well fed, lusty stallions, each neighing for another man's wife." It seems to me an uncanny description of our own time.

In the summer of 1987, a promising political candidate was forced from the field when his alleged adulterous behavior came to light. How surprising that in our permissive society, a society in which promiscuity and sexual license have long been the norm, the hue and cry over his indiscretion would result in such public outrage. Adultery may be acceptable in a TV soap opera, but it is not readily accepted in a candidate for the highest office in our land.

In the Old Testament, the words "adultery" and "idolatry" are used interchangeably, and that makes sense. The sex drive, unchecked and unrestrained, becomes very much like idolatry. Our own desires get out of hand and reason leaves. We simply have to have her/him. We don't care about the consequences. Our passions become our god, and God Himself is no longer Lord of our lives. Our own sexual fulfillment becomes our idol.

Adultery is a sin against self. We read that, "But a man who commits adultery lacks judgement; whoever does so destroys himself" (Proverbs 6:32). God has paid the ultimate price, the blood of His Son, to redeem us. He has good plans for us. To ignore that love and those plans in order to indulge our appetites, is to take that first step down the path of self-deception and, ultimately, self-hate and self-destruction. It leads to the erosion of all our honorable intentions and all our feelings of self-worth.

About twenty years ago, a book called *Open Marriage* by George and Nena O'Neal caused a stir. In an open marriage, the partners ought not to be constrained by total commitment to each other. Those limitations prevent individual fulfillment. That was the premise of the book, and it was highly successful. More recently, a new book of theirs retracts that advice. Old-fashioned virtues of loyalty and fidelity are once more promoted. Sociology, it seems, has caught up with the Bible.

One woman told me recently, "I've been through three intense relationships already. Now I just want to try something uncomplicated like getting married." Unfortunately, marriage is not without complications. Any commitment extracts a price. Commitment to Jesus Christ is not easy. To give yourself to another person in an unbreakable covenant is not easy. The difficulties seem sometimes to outweigh the rewards. Over two thousand years ago, Socrates gave his pupils this advice: "By all means marry. If you get a good wife, you'll become very happy. If you get a bad one, you will become a philosopher, and that is good for every man."

The apostle Paul, in his letter to the Corinthians, urges them to fulfill their marital duties. "The wife's body does not belong to her alone, but also to her husband. In the same way, the husband's body does not belong to him alone, but also to his wife. Do not deprive each other except by mutual consent and for a time, so that you might devote yourselves to prayer. Then come together again so that Satan will not tempt you" (1 Corinthians 7:4–5). In depriving our partner of normal sexual relations, we may drive that partner to sexual immorality and adultery.

An old rhyme proposes that "It's better to have loved and lost than to marry a girl you can't defrost." But it is just as frustrating to marry a man you can't defrost and, from years of counseling couples, I am aware that is not uncommon. Your marriage vows put you under an obligation to be attractive and exciting and fulfilling to your partner. Their very chastity may depend on it.

The giving or witholding of sex within a marriage is just one of the power games we often play. Gert Behanna touched on this in her book, *The Late Liz.* It is the story of her conversion at about age sixty. Prior to that, she was a wealthy, privileged lady and three times married. She had tried everything—alcohol, drugs, even suicide, before God came into her life. But she gives this interesting description of her sex life. Her first husband was a sexual athlete, and she spent most of her years with him running around the bedroom trying to avoid him. The second time around, she prayed that the Lord would send her a "quiet harbor." In that marriage she felt denied, unloved, sexually frustrated. In her words, "I never knew how quiet a harbor could be."

Gert's story, I think, reveals a perverseness familiar to most. Our sexual needs are determined by our partner's appetites or lack of them. A panting, eager partner is met with indifference, and an indifferent partner drives his or her mate to ever-increasing sexual demands. It is a power game for both parties, and with God's help you can change that game. As we try more and more to be the person our partner needs, he or she may become the person that we need.

Even within the framework of a happy and satisfying marriage there are, of course, temptations to immorality and lust. Jimmy Carter, when he was president, gave an interview in which he confessed to "having lusted in my heart for a few women." A friend of mine commented on reading that, "Only a few? What a piker!" But the more I learn about Jimmy Carter, the less I believe he lusted in his heart after any woman. He was talking about being tempted, and there is a big difference between temptation and lust. I doubt that any healthy man or woman with normal sexual desires will ever come to a place in life where attractive persons of the opposite sex go totally unnoticed, I know I haven't come to that place. I may even muse to myself, "Lord, isn't she lovely?" The Lord will say, "Yes, I know. I made her, but she's not for you. Be about your business." That's typical and normal temptation and we are never free of it.

The Bible tells us that Jesus did not sin, but that He was tempted in every way just as we are. On those cold nights in the Galileean hills when nothing was going right and the disciples were bickering, don't you suppose he was full of doubts and unknown yearnings? Did he sometimes wish that one of those lovely women, Mary or Martha or someone else, would just hold Him in her arms and dispel the fears and loneliness? If He was tempted like us in all things, that's not unlikely. But lust goes farther than temptation. Lust is the result of harboring that temptation, nurturing it and making plans around it. When you've gone that far, you might as well commit the act, according to Jesus.

The only way to avoid either temptation or lust is to walk in the light. We are all vulnerable, but pastors are, I believe, especially so, and I remind our pastoral staff of that. They enter into intimate emotional relationships with people who are needy, who are desperate for love and acceptance. There is always a possibility of sexual temptation and of moving out of the professional role into a personal one.

The answer to sexual temptation is not cold showers and prayer. Psychologists tell us that if the will and the imagination are in conflict, the imagination wins every time. We cannot simply make up our minds to be pure. We need to be open and accountable, to have a handful of people in our lives to whom we can confess our temptations and thereby diffuse their power over us. Jesus has promised that, "Where two or three are gathered, there am I in the midst." As we expose those dark secrets to His healing light in prayer with a few of the faithful, they can disappear like snow in summer.

In that same letter to the Corinthians, Paul says, "flee from sexual immorality. All other sins a man commits are outside his body, but he who sins sexually sins against his own body."

Those of us who are married are to help our partners avoid sexual immorality, or adultery. Avoid minimizing that partner. Don't be like the wife whose husband suggested they play Trivial Pursuit. "Why should I?" she replied, "I already caught you." Those little digs are sometimes said teasingly, but, over the years, they have the effect of undermining our partners' confidence and feelings of worth, and even the ability to perform sexually.

Above all, be a priest, the one who stands between your beloved and Jesus, saying, doing, being God's love to that person.

One final word. If you are now or have been an adulterer, is that the worst sin you can commit? The answer is no. It is a sin against God, against your partner and yourself. But it is difficult to measure the extent to which breaking the seventh commandment is or isn't more serious than breaking the other nine. Sin is whatever separates us from God. Hear this: Jesus loves us, adulterers or not. Jesus died for us, adulterers or not. All have sinned and fall short of the glory of God. And He has provided a way out in Jesus Christ.

16. Yours and Mine

I dare say most of us have stolen something at least once in our lives. Whenever and whatever it was for you, I'll bet the incident is still vivid in your mind. You may have stolen change from your mother's purse, coins out of the Sunday school collection, supplies from school, or a toy from a friend. In my case, it was a comic book.

I was in the third grade at the time and running with a wild sort of gang, the leader of which was a kid named Jimmie. One fateful afternoon, Jimmie offered to take me down and show me how to appropriate what I wanted at Woolworth's on Howard Street. Consequently, I was introduced to the world of shoplifting, in this case of Big-Little Books, the precursor of today's comic books. To my horror, Jimmie was caught. The manager held him in custody while I was sent back to tell his parents what had happened and to ask them to come and pick him up. It was two miles back to the apartment building where Jimmie and I lived, and I ran all the way, knees shaking. I stopped once to throw up. I'll never forget knocking on the apartment door and announcing to these two bewildered people that Jimmie was being held in custody at Woolworth's. I was overcome with shame and guilt.

Those memories are still vivid, I guess, because we were a lot healthier in those days. We had a clear sense of right and wrong, and we instinctively knew when we had done something wrong. That's a good thing to know. We may think that we have never stolen anything since those early, furtive excursions into crime. We're probably deceiving ourselves. Unfortunately, adulthood and sophistication are usually accompanied by a searing of conscience whereby we can no longer distinguish between what is ours and what is somebody else's.

In 1529, Martin Luther commented on this prevailing human condition. He said, "If all who are thieves, though they are unwilling to admit it, were hanged on the gallows, the world would soon be empty, and there would be a shortage of both hangmen and gallows." The Bible assumes that you and I are, by nature, law-breakers, and commandment number eight, "Thou shalt not steal," is just one of the laws we break, or bend a little. To recognize that is the only way back to forgiveness, restitution, and repentance.

Those four words, "Thou shalt not steal," seem supremely clear. There is no fine print, no clause, and no room for misrepresentation. Yet, the Old Testament Jews had 2,748 learned commentaries on just this one commandment. There were 4,801 different interpretations of its meaning and more than 5,000 exceptions to its simple rule.

It is still sometimes difficult to define stealing. A man was riding in a taxi in a strange city when he realized he had left his wallet back in the hotel room. A way out occurred to him, and he asked the driver to pull over at the next drugstore. "I want to buy some matches," he explained. "I just dropped a $50 bill on the floor of your cab and can't seem to find it." As you might expect, when he came out of the drugstore, the cab was gone. We might need those 4,801 interpretations mentioned above to determine which of those two men was most guilty of breaking the eighth commandment.

In this matter of honesty, we are given to applying different standards to others than we do to ourselves. God's clear command becomes a matter of interpretation. Many of us are like George Gershwin, prolific composer of a generation ago. Gershwin, I'm told, was convinced that every piece of music he ever wrote was magnificent, and he was certain that everybody else shared that opinion. He played a new composition for a friend one day and asked for an opinion. His friend made a face. "It's not up to your standard, George. As a matter of fact, you've never done worse. The melody is weak and monotonous. Take my advice—tear it up and start all over." There was a long silence after which Gershwin continued, "Now give me your honest opinion." God has said, "You shall not steal." We tend to think He meant to qualify that. But there are no loopholes. You are supposed to know the difference between yours and mine, yours and somebody else's.

In the twentieth century there are many opportunities to break the eighth commandment in ways that may seem inconsequential, even harmless. Cheating on our tax returns is one of those. We don't want to recognize that we are cheating every other citizen who is then required to shoulder an even greater share of the tax burden. It's fair game, we think, to cheat an insurance company by claiming, for example, whiplash, a claim hard to disprove. In reality, every other person insured by that company will eventually pay for our fraud.

Plagiarism, stealing someone else's words or ideas, has often been a difficult-to-prove crime. Louis L'Amour, the prolific author of westerns, had that experience. A collection of his earlier stories was recently published under someone else's name. He can't sue, because he forgot to copyright them. Supposedly, you can't steal something that nobody owns. That may be a legitimate legal defense; but, in the eyes of God, the guilty party may just as well have picked Louis L'Amour's pocket.

Occasionally, in the downtown areas of my city, I've watched people steal newspapers off the stands. I'm astonished that they will break the eighth commandment for a 25 cents newspaper. I tend to feel very smug until I remember some of my own misdeeds. In college, somebody in our dorm discovered a way to make a penny do the work of a dime in our phone booths. (A call cost ten cents back in those dim and dark ages.) I can't tell you the number of times I broke the eighth commandment to save nine cents. If I had any qualms, I rationalized them. "Why should I pay a dime when everybody else was paying a penny?" In the end, we were all punished. The phone company, disgusted by all that cheating, removed the phone entirely.

Stealing from an employer is a common, easily rationalized form of stealing. A friend tells a wonderful story on this subject about his mother-in-law. She was a widow who raised two daughters. In their teens, each of the girls got a summer job, one as a waitress at Howard Johnson's and the other as a secretary. The first girl started bringing ice cream home for the family—courtesy of Howard Johnson's, though her employers didn't know about that. The other boasted frequently that she hadn't had to buy any pads or pencils since she started her job. She just helped herself to office supplies. Their mother was distressed about both situations and one day confronted them. "Listen, girls, this is stealing." "Oh Mom, you don't understand," they assured her. "This goes with the job. Everybody takes home a few things from inventory." "Really?" said their mom. "Suppose I told you that I was planning to take home a few things from inventory?" Mom was a bank manager. The girls got the message. Purloining a few things from inventory is a minor or major crime, depending on the inventory. But, in either event, it is stealing.

I was part of a college mission team when I was in seminary. Four of us would hit the eastern campuses on the weekends, knock on dorm doors, hold meetings and witness. God blessed that effort far beyond our own abilities. I still remember a weekend at Westminster College in Pennsylvania when one of the star athletes decided to become a Christian. He played several sports and excelled in most of them. As a result of his decision he realized he had been breaking the eighth commandment for a long time. With two or three friends from his dorm, he carried back all the stuff he had stolen from the athletic department over the years—shoes, sweat shirts, equipment of all kinds. You can imagine the impact on the campus when that story got around.

There are, however, other forms of stealing not as obvious as those we have been talking about. Laziness is one of them, particularly in any group project. When the pilgrims first came to our shores they set up a form of government that we would call communistic. They had all things in common. That lasted until Governor Bradford discovered that there was gold-bricking, malingering, parasitism, and absenteeism among the colonists. In 1623, he changed the rules. Each man had to grow the food for his own family or they would go hungry. It worked. He wrote later, "All hands became industrious, and any want and famine has not been among us from that day." When you don't pull your weight, do your share, you're stealing.

Denying a worker a fair wage is a form of theft. Our daughter is an attorney for the Rural Legal Services in Florida and has done extensive work among migrant workers, some of them illegal aliens. She is especially passionate on this subject. Illegal migrants have no rights and are exploited by their employers. But even legal farm-workers work long hours for little money and are housed, too often, in substandard conditions. In the last analysis, they are the victims of theft.

Dishonest advertising is stealing. Government agencies protect us from the worst excesses, but we are still bombarded with outrageous claims for one product or another. I was told about a veterinarian who was treating a horse for a limp. "It's strange," confided the horse's owner. "He limps one day and then doesn't limp the next. What should I do?" The vet had the perfect solution. "Sell him on the day he doesn't limp."

Even professional people have been known to cross the line between fair recompense and robbery. Unnecessary surgery, of which we are told there is a goodly amount these days, is stealing—not just money but emotional, physical well-being. In a local clinic, a doctor was overheard asking, "If I find an operation necessary, do you have the money to pay for it?" "If I don't have the money to pay for it," responded the patient, "will you find an operation necessary?"

Lawyers are periodically under attack for unethical, money-grabbing tactics that may or may not be covered by the eighth commandment. I happen to have a son and daughter both of whom are lawyers, so I need to tread carefully here. But I'll share one story. A certain lawyer arrived in heaven and was met with a good deal of excitement. "We've been waiting for you. There's going to be a great celebration in your honor." The newcomer was bewildered and asked the reason for all this. "You're the oldest person ever to have lived since Methuselah. You're 186 years old, aren't you?" "No, certainly not." "But we've added up your time sheets," his welcomer exclaimed, "the hours you've charged your clients for. That's how old we figure you must be." Actually, it is not my intention to impugn any one profession. The point is, every time we take money we haven't earned, whatever we do for a living, we are stealing.

When our daughter was about twelve years old, she accompanied her grandmother on a trip to Hong Kong. My mother had supported two children in that city for many years, and the older boy was graduating from high school. Grandma and Chris went as part of a group from a very conservative, evangelical college in the Midwest—all of them singing hymns and reading their Bibles daily along the way and witnessing to Chris about their faith. As the trip ended and it was time to clear customs, other less admirable qualities emerged. Most of the passengers were bragging about the way they had been able to beat the system—to bring in all their expensive Hong Kong purchases without paying duty. Their theft was all a game, but a game that dealt a damaging blow to the faith of a twelve-year-old.

Theft is considered a serious crime throughout the Old Testament. Four of the prophets, Ezekiel, Zechariah, Isaiah, and Amos mention this particular sin. God had chosen the Israelites as the people from whom He would bless the world. This new society was to be founded on righteousness. Integrity and honesty were essential building blocks, as God shaped a new nation. But in breaking the eighth commandment, we also sin against our neighbor. Stealing his property, we steal part of his life. He has given an honest day's work for wages and used those wages to buy goods. I defraud my neighbor when I steal his property, his rightful recompense for his investment of time, energy and talent.

Above all, stealing is a sin against God. It goes without saying that those who are serious about their faith will not even be tempted by the more blatant forms of theft. But we can rationalize or waffle on the more subtle practices we have been talking about in regard to the IRS, the customs office, our employer, or clients. When we do that, we reveal a basic lack of trust in God's ability to provide for our needs. We start looking out for ourselves and for our own interests.

Our understanding of all ten commandments, has been considerably muddied by the advent of situational ethics. Its proponents challenge the necessity for and reality of ethical absolutes. They would say that all moral behavior is contextual and must be judged in the light of the accompanying circumstances. For example, is Robin Hood a thief or a hero? The fact that he stole is not the issue. He took from the rich to give to the poor. Therefore, he committed no crime, according to the situational ethics people. His motivation is taken into account and waters down the absolute of God's command.

With that premise, I can move on to justify all sorts of things such as theft at my job. I can take not only pencils and paperclips, tools and equipment, but even hours off on the basis that my employers have, in one way or another, been stealing from me. I am underpaid. My true worth is not recognized. The boss's son got the promotion I deserved. My stealing is not really a crime. I'm just taking what is due me. As one pursues that line of reasoning, a lot of questionable behavior is excusable.

Our newspapers recently reported a strange theft in our city's botanical gardens. An elderly couple, both dressed in evening clothes, were observed driving up in their Mercedes Benz. They got out, proceeded to cut great armfuls of the choicest flowers, stowed them in their car, and drove off. It's possible that it did not occur to them that they were stealing. After all, it's a public park and they are taxpayers, and, obviously, the botanical gardens have more flowers than they need. In that context, their behavior is perfectly justified.

Then there are situations where the honorable course is simply too much trouble. There is the occasional heartwarming story of a taxpayer who made some error in his return inadvertently twenty years ago. Now he wants to send in the five dollars he owes, oblivious to the fact that far more than five dollars of taxpayers' money will be required to straighten the situation out.

I love the story of the carpetlayer who was caught in a moral dilemma. He was installing wall-to-wall carpeting in a home, and when he finished he reached for a cigarette pack and found it missing. At the same time, he noticed a slight bump in the middle of the carpet. Should he rip up the carpet and retract the package? That would be the honest thing to do, but much too time-consuming. Instead, he got a two by four and tapped the bump until it was flattened. Later, back in his car, two things happened simultaneously. He found his pack of cigarettes lying on the seat, and the lady of the house came running toward him, obviously distressed. "Yoo hoo mister, have you seen my parakeet anywhere?" A grisly story, but still an example of those sticky situations where we are caught between a quick solution and an honest one.

I began this chapter with a premise that we have all broken the eighth commandment. Our sin is just a matter of degree, whether we have stolen a newspaper or some senior citizen's life savings. We can repent, make restitution, and find God's love and grace. God says through Zechariah, "I will that nobody be lost. I don't take pleasure in the death of the wicked." Ezekiel says, "None of the sins that he has committed shall be remembered against him. He has done what is lawful and right. He shall surely live." Whichever one of God's laws we break, we are to admit it, try to make it right and believe that we are forgiven. Corey Ten Boom, that colorful Dutch Christian and author of *The Hiding Place,* was fond of saying it this way: "Bury your sins in the deepest part of the ocean and hang a sign there that says, 'No Fishing.'"

In 1930, during the Great Depression, a man named Golden Rule Jones was mayor of Toledo, Ohio. During his term of office, he sometimes sat as the presiding judge in night court.

One night a man was brought in for stealing money from a grocery store. His defense was that he needed the money for food and that he was simply a victim of hard times. Nevertheless, Golden Rule Jones found him guilty. "You did not steal from society," he said. "You stole from a private citizen and you broke the law. I'm fining you ten dollars. However," and he reached for his wallet, "I'll pay it for you." Next he instructed the bailiff to pass the hat around the courtroom. "I'm fining everybody here at least fifty cents. You're all guilty of being members of a society that made it necessary for this man to steal. The collection will go to the defendant."

In Golden Rule Jones's courtroom, justice was tempered with mercy. To me, that's just a glimpse of the treatment we can expect at the hands of our heavenly Father. Whatever our sin, we have an advocate, Jesus Christ, who has promised us forgiveness and new life.

17. So Help Me God

My wife is addicted to courtroom drama. She was an avid fan of *Perry Mason*. Lives are hanging in the balance, and the moment finally comes when the definitive witness takes the stand to prove Perry's client innocent. We wait breathlessly while, first of all, the oath is taken. "I swear to tell the truth, the whole truth, and nothing but the truth, so help me God." At stake is the premise that as a nation or individual we believe in the ninth commandment. Telling the truth is the foundation of the judicial system.

I have been guilty of passing on terrible lawyer jokes, like the one about the research facility that is presently testing lawyers instead of white mice because there are so many more of them, and you don't get so attached to them. But, on a serious note, the lawyers I know, some of whom are family members, or good and honored friends, are conscientious, dedicated men and women, working toward justice and equality for all citizens.

The numbers of young people pursuing a vocation in law today are staggering. As a nation, we are engaged in litigation far in excess of any other nation in the world. I think those statistics indicate that our judicial system is perhaps the most honored institution in our land, far more honored than the church, unfortunately, or than business or government or even medicine, though for so long doctors have been the high priests of our society. The system is flawed, of course. It is slow and justice and truth do not always prevail. But it is still the finest system ever devised. People with no other recourse turn to the law because they believe it is their best chance to have their grievances heard. The legal system is trusted, and it should be.

The ninth commandment concerns bearing false witness, and that is directly tied in to the legal system. Truth is the backbone of that system, and without truth the system fails and with it the whole fabric of society. Those who purjure themselves are seriously penalized, as they should be. We have said that the last six commandments zero in on how to love our neighbor as ourself, and this ninth commandment provides an important key to loving our neighbors within a society.

The ninth commandment was originally given to the Hebrews when they were a nomadic people. When the law was handed down, they were to wander forty more years in the wilderness before they would have any settled kind of community life. That lifestyle reduced the options in dealing with criminals found guilty by their peers. There was no portable jail to carry from place to place in the desert. There were just two options for handling lawbreakers. In one, the guilty party made restitution—not a bad way to go even today with white-collar crime. Why pay $16,000 a year to confine people who ought to be out working to repay what they've stolen? Restitution was a solution in non-violent crimes, but more serious offenses resulted in the death penalty.

With that tradition, we appreciate the importance of this commandment. A false witness was likely to condemn someone to death in those primitive times. False witness was akin to murder, and that made the Israelites especially cautious. No one could be condemned solely on the evidence of one witness. For conviction in a crime requiring the death sentence, at least two witnesses had to agree and, further, they must be eye witnesses. But there is a larger framework in which we need to examine the ninth commandment. Whether or not we are ever under oath in a courtroom, a lie, any lie, is wrong. There are hundreds of verses and chapters in both Old and New Testaments that deal with the sin of lying.

I was thinking about the definition of a lie as it pertains to a twentieth-century man or woman living in the Western world. I came up with a whole list of definitions of blatant or subtle lies, black or white lies, deliberate or casual lies. Incidentally, I am not necessarily listing these in order of their seriousness.

First of all, there is malicious lying. We know it is an untruth, and we say it anyway, simply because of something perverse and evil at work in us. Satan has been called the Father of Lies, and I happen to believe that all lies are the result of his work within us. God, as we know, is truth; and when we maliciously and deliberately lie, we align ourselves with the ultimate enemy.

We lie by boasting. Why do we find it necessary to make ourselves look smarter, braver, more admirable than we are? We are usually covering our inferiority feelings. We who are chosen, loved, redeemed, can still have those feelings of worthlessness, of low self-esteem. Those boasting lies are born of fear. They are aimed at lowering the stress level. But they have the opposite effect. By our grandiosity, we put impossible demands on ourselves. In a less serious vein, I recently read some suggestions about when and when not to exaggerate: (1) Do not exaggerate when performing neurosurgery; (2) in writing military dispatches before the battle; (3) on job applications; (4) when running a bureau of the budget; (5) in marriage. On the other hand, exaggeration may be helpful (1) in lovemaking and courtship; (2) in leading a cavalry charge; (3) when speaking at funerals; (4) when defending a murderer; (5) in military dispatches after the battle; (6) in political speeches; (7) when writing thank-you notes.

Gossip is a form of lying. It is careless character assassination. We pass on malicious stories that may destroy someone else's life and reputation. It is an especially nasty form of lying. It is bearing false witness under casual, social circumstances, whereby we cannot even be held accountable for the damage we do.

Then there are the white lies, the social lies. I have a hunch that in this matter God is color blind. The white ones and the black ones look the same. These white lies are often the result of our pathetic attempts to say, "Please love me; please love me." The lies I tell about you or about me are aimed at making you like me more.

I have been guilty of that kind of lying. My wife loves to remind me about one particularly embarrassing example. In our first parish, a kindly couple had invited us for dinner. They had both been born in the Middle East, and they prepared an ethnic meal in our honor, with many and varied dishes. One of them seemed, to these two Americans, almost inedible, though we tried valiantly. To hide my true feelings about this particular dish, I began to rave about it. "Isn't this wonderful? I love it." My wife glared at me. We lived there for three more years, and at least once a month our hostess appeared at our door with a huge bowl of this inedible stuff, convinced that I loved it. On each of those occasions, my wife would take me to task. "Do you see what you've done? When are you going to quit telling those white lies?"

We can lie by our silence. A false impression is conveyed, simply because we didn't say anything. Our silence could simply be a way of avoiding involvement. Interestingly enough, in Jewish law, the person who kept silent and withheld the truth was as guilty as a liar. If you can speak up to protect a reputation or change the course of events or exonerate someone else, do so. Otherwise, your very silence is a form of lying.

We lie by half-truths, which are also half-lies. Abraham, the man of faith and father of the faithful, told a few of those. He was in Egypt with his beautiful wife and fearful that Pharaoh would seize her and have him killed. He devised a scheme. He would tell Pharaoh that Sarah was his sister, which she actually was—a half-sister. He didn't add, however, that she was also his wife. His half-truth turned out to be a total lie, and he was caught by it.

We lie to ourselves which is the basis of a good deal of emotional and psychological problems. Years ago a friend of mine turned my life around in this area. He said, "Bruce, do you know what's wrong with you? You judge other people by their actions and yourself by your intentions. However you have hurt someone else, you are never guilty. You always mean to do the right thing. Why don't you reverse that, and judge other people by their intentions, which are seldom malicious, and judge yourself by your actions?" That is what holy living is all about—to stop justifying our own actions and to cease lying about our good intentions.

Finally, we can lie to God. Cain did. God asked him the whereabouts of his brother whom he had just killed, and he said, "How should I know? Am I my brother's keeper?" I don't think very many of us would lie to God so cheekily, but that in itself indicates a strange state of affairs. We are more afraid of the opinions and actions of other people than we are of God's. We lie to others to impress them, to please them. We are not as likely to lie to God because His judgments seem remote, His presence less real.

Lying in any of the above forms is, first of all, against God's clear commandment. In a courtroom, as we said, witnesses vow to tell the truth, "so help me God." That is an awesome oath. To lie in the face of such an oath is to put your soul in eternal jeopardy. God is truth, and all lies are contradictory to His will.

Our lies can destroy our neighbors. Our gossip, our half-truths, our withholding of the truth, all leave a trail of victims in their wake. It might be worthwhile to touch just a little bit here on a pervasive problem of our society, the lies and distortions of the media and the power they have to shape our lives and our opinions. Polls have shown that only 8 percent of the people who write and disseminate our news attend church at all. The other 92 percent are nonchurch members. That could account for some of the distortions we observe in stories about the church or the Christian cause.

For example, the Pope's visit to Nicaragua was often inaccurately reported. At one televised mass, the Sandanista government kept the front pews for their own officials. Most of the Nicaraguans seemed thrilled by the Pope's visit. They came to mass in great numbers to cheer and cry and pray, but only the officials in the front row were televised. Audiences all over the world watched people shaking their fists and booing and jeering during the mass—the reaction of a tiny fraction of the congregation.

In response to the protest from the front rows, the Pope would raise the crucifix and say, "I offer you the love and grace of Jesus Christ." The mass itself was said in the Mesquite dialect. The Pope was well aware that the Sandanistas had murdered thousands of Mesquite Indians. He spoke the language of the murdered to their murderers. The press, in commenting on this, said he spoke some unknown dialect to a hostile crowd. This kind of reporting, intentional or accidental, ignores the Christian witness of the faithful majority and turns the incident into a political confrontation.

We are increasingly skeptical about the truthfulness of our nation's leaders. Polls indicate that three-quarters of our citizens believe the government lies to them. They have reason to. Even President Eisenhower, a beloved general and grandfather figure, lied about the existence of the U-2 surveillance planes. The lies about the true situation in Viet Nam continued for more than a decade. A government with the obligation to set the standards of truth for the whole nation, has done us all a disservice. There is righteousness and justice in the land only when truth prevails.

Christians are to keep the ninth commandment because we in the new covenant are still under the law, according to Jesus. By His own admission, He did not come to change any part of the law. But there is a law that supercedes all ten of the commandments, including this one of bearing false witness or lying. The royal law of agape love is our higher commandment, according to Jesus. "Love one another, as I have loved you."

Let's examine some ways in which that higher law might conflict with this ninth commandment. Just suppose a man came rushing into my office some morning, waving a gun and demanding the whereabouts of another staff member. Certainly I wouldn't tell him the truth. I would probably say, "I don't know," even if I did. I might say nothing, or I might tell a bolder lie—"He's left town." You see, the royal law of love says I am to protect my friend from harm and prevent a disturbed person from carrying out a crime. In the best interest of both, I am going to lie and lie and lie.

The royal law of love also releases us from having to tell everybody the truth about everything we think or know. When I stand in the narthex on Sunday mornings, I don't want to hear that I just preached the most boring sermon ever, even if it is true. I have relieved my parishioners of that obligation. They might say, "Bruce, I loved *last* Sunday's sermon" (or one six months ago); I'll get the message. You don't have to tell your boss that he's difficult. You don't have to tell your mother-in-law she's nasty. Some truths can be left unsaid. At one point, even the Bible seems to justify lying. The Hebrew midwives were told to kill every male Hebrew child they delivered. When Pharaoh inquires about why that had not been done, they replied that the Hebrew women were so strong that babies arrived before the midwives could get there. That was a lie, one required under the royal law of love.

Even the truth can be used to deceive. *The Yearling* is the story of a group of mountain people whose prize possessions are their bear dogs. One of the characters, Penny Baxter, has a worthless dog he wants to sell to his neighbor. Traditionally, every man told outrageous lies about his dog's abilities, his faithfulness, his aggressiveness. Baxter tells Len, his neighbor, that the dog is a mess, "he ain't worth a good twist of tobaccy . . . sorriest bear dog I ever followed." Len has never heard anybody talk that way about their dog. The next day he arrives at Penny's house demanding to buy the dog. He'll give his best shotgun for him. The trade is made. Later, Penny suffers an attack of conscience and he tells his son that he feels bad about what he did. His son says, "You told the truth, Pa." "My words was straight," agrees Penny, "but my intention was as crooked as the Oklawaha River." We can all find clever ways to deceive ourselves and others, not just by lies, but with truth. Ultimately, it is our intent that is at issue.

We have made a case for lying in the higher cause of love, but in one area lying is never the right course—lying to ourselves. This is what walking in the light is all about. Every revival in the last two thousand years was touched off when the Spirit of God began to prod believers to walk in the light, and to confess their sins—past and present. All the hidden lies and hatreds and deceptions are brought into God's healing light. "If we confess our sins, he is faithful and just and will forgive us our sins and purify us from all unrighteousness" (1 John 1:9). On the few occasions when young preachers ask my advice about the pastorate, I always suggest they tell people about their sins right at the outset. They are going to be found out anyway. I urge them to tell the congregation, or at least the church officers, those places where their faith journey is and has been difficult. Disarm them. In that climate of openness, God's Spirit will surely do a great work.

If we want to be obedient to the ninth commandment, the first step is simple. Call a lie a lie. A woman came to Dwight Moody years ago, asking, "How can I stop my little boy from telling fibs?" "To begin with," he said, "call them lies." We all fall into those innocuous euphemisms that take the onus out of our misdeeds. We don't lie, we "stretch the truth." We don't lie, we "have a memory lapse." We don't lie, we "protect" the other person. We don't lie, we are just selective about the facts.

In contrast to all those evasive manipulations of the facts in the cause of expediency or self-interest, God's mandate is clear and simple: Tell the truth, the whole truth, and nothing but the truth, so help us God.

18. Looking Over the Fence

The tenth commandment is the one that shatters all our illusions about righteousness. Up to this point, many of us have probably been feeling a little smug. As far as we know, we have kept all nine of the preceding commandments. But is there anyone who has never coveted, has never looked over the neighbor's fence and envied his or her green grass, wonderful marriage, social position, great job, successful children, looks, talents? Is there anyone who can claim he or she has never envied someone else, what they have or what they are?

Some years ago when we lived in Maryland we had an experience I would covet for all of us. When our older children were starting college, we moved into a neighborhood of young marrieds and young singles. Our car was a little newer, our house a bit bigger, and our vacations a little more luxurious. We were "the Joneses," the people to keep up with. It's a strange feeling. Prior to that, we had lived in neighborhoods surrounded by a good many better-off folks, and felt somewhat deprived that we couldn't do what they did, or have what they had.

But even if you are the Joneses, the media will erode your sense of well-being. Those who think they are at the top of the heap have only to watch a show called "Lifestyles of the Rich and Famous" in order to feel discontented and envious. You may think you are fairly affluent until you get a look at how the really privileged people live with houses abroad, sports cars, private planes. Shows like "Dallas" and "Dynasty" present a posh lifestyle as if it were the usual American lifestyle, and that is the conclusion drawn by people all over the world as they watch those shows—and, believe me, they do. We were crossing a desert area in Israel on one occasion and commented on the incongruous sight of Bedouin tents sporting TV aerials. "They're probably watching 'Dallas,'" commented our guide. "That's the leading show around here."

Let's start, then, with the assumption that it is impossible to keep this last commandment. It is the hardest one because it deals with attitude while the other nine commandments prohibit or encourage certain behaviors, specific acts,—don't steal, don't kill, keep the Sabbath, honor your father and mother. It is far more difficult to change our attitudes than our behavior. We are faced with the task of reversing long-held perceptions about ourselves and the world around us. Someone has said, "We often feel guilty for what we do, seldom for what we are."

An Episcopal canon from Canada, Quentin Warner, used a phrase to describe the problem, one that has stuck with me over the years. "Don't be surprised when people do what they do. When they have been changed to what they ought to be, but are not, they will do what they ought to have done, but could not." The key to behavioral change is a conversion of the heart and mind and will.

If I could give you the gift of being able to keep just one commandment perfectly, I'd choose number ten. If you don't covet what is your neighbor's in any way, you will not be tempted to break any of the four preceding commandments. You won't kill or commit adultery. You won't steal or bear false witness. All those crimes are rooted in enmity toward our neighbor, an enmity born of covetousness more often than not. The intent of this tenth commandment, in blunt terms, is this: God wants to do some slum clearance. That slum is inside of you and me. He wants to get rid of those decaying, rat-infested buildings out of which come evil, antisocial behavior. He wants to give us a new heart and attitude, and there is no better place to begin this radical project than with the tenth commandment. Do not covet.

Covetousness is more than merely looking over my neighbor's fence. It is lusting after what he or she is and has. That basic envy translates into enmity and mean-spiritedness toward my neighbor until, inevitably, unloving actions follow. Covetousness is not just temptation. To be tempted means we look over the fence and comment, maybe a little ruefully, on his superior state. "Gosh, he has green grass. I wish mine looked like that." That's OK. When you move from that to resenting that he has it and you don't, maybe even plotting to get what your neighbor has, you are coveting.

As we have said, all ten of these commandments were given to a bronze-age nomadic people through God's spokesman, Moses. The things they were not to covet were carefully itemized. Don't covet your neighbor's house, which really meant household. They had no permanent homes. Your household consisted of all the things you could pack on the backs of your animals—your tent, lampstand, bowls and cooking utensils, clothing and ornaments. The household was entirely portable. Don't covet your neighbor's wife. That's self-explanatory. It means today exactly what it meant then. Don't covet your neighbor's ox and ass, the primary possessions of these nomadic people. They were essential in moving the household from place to place. We could compare it to coveting our neighbor's car. Don't covet your neighbor's manservant or maidservant. And, finally, the all-inclusive phrase, don't covet *anything* that belongs to your neighbor.

The Old Testament provides sobering stories about the evils of coveting. Just forty years after the commandments were given, a new generation of Israelites under Joshua's leadership were going to finally claim the land that God had promised them. They were to cross the Jordan and prepare to take the great fortified city of Jericho. God gave them the victory. Simply by marching around the walls seven times and blowing horns, they conquered the city. Later, in a battle for Ai, a much smaller and less-fortified city, they were defeated. They had been instructed to take no booty or loot, and one man disobeyed, a man named Achen. Achen confessed that he coveted a man's gold and silver and wrapped it up and buried it under his tent. The battle was lost because one man coveted.

Then there was, of course, King David, who coveted his neighbor's wife. David, the man after God's own heart, caught sight of Bathsheba bathing on a rooftop and was consumed with desire for her. He sent for her, even though he was told she was the wife of one of his officers. Later on, when he learned she was pregnant, he managed to have her husband, Uriah, killed. The problems that befell the nation of Israel and the household of King David because of that one act of coveting were many.

We are no longer a nomadic people, and the list of things we are not to covet would be a good deal different in our time. We still have houses and households, but few of us have maidservants or manservants, and even fewer have an ox or an ass. But let's think about the modern equivalents of some of those things.

We have already mentioned coveting our neighbor's affluence, social position, or job, but we can covet some less tangible things, such as youth or health. We resent getting old in a world that seems increasingly physically fit and active—jogging, playing raquetball and tennis. Failing health seems like an unfair blow. "Why me, Lord?" "Why did I get cancer?" "Why does my husband have a stroke?" "Why does my son have AIDS?" Our self-pity moves into resentment and anger at all those happy-go-lucky well people in the world.

It seems more and more of the population covets thinness. Those of us on the pudgy side have a hard time with the forever-thin people, born with the proper metabolism. The plain are forever envious of the beautiful, the small of stature of the tall. The bald covet those with full heads of hair.

But, like the Israelites, we continue to covet our neighbor's husband or wife. We are sure we got a lemon in the grab-bag of life. "If I only had his wife . . . life would be so much more exciting and fulfilling." There are married people who envy single people, jealous of their freedom or their open choices, wishing they had a second chance. Single people envy the married. They would trade all that freedom for a stable and enduring relationship of love. At the root of envy is this premise: "Whatever somebody else has, it's better than mine. I got shortchanged." We may not consciously think the world owes us a living, but, as one man remarked, it could say, "'I'm sorry.'"

Covetousness is at the root of original sin, the sin of Adam and Eve in the Garden of Eden. Genesis gives us an account of man's eternal primal problem. The first man and woman have everything. They have each other. All their needs are met. They have a garden to walk in and, in which God, their friend, walks with them each evening. Then the tempter appears. He tells them they don't really have it all. God has been keeping something from them, something they are entitled to. If they will just eat of the fruit of the forbidden tree, they will be like God. They will have everything He has, know everything He knows. It is a powerful enticement—irresistible, in fact. Coveting God's wisdom and power, they break the one rule He had given them and lose their place in Paradise.

Philosophers over the centuries understood the problem. Five hundred years before the birth of our Lord, Heroditus said, "Envy is born in a man from the start." At about the same time in history, Aeschylus wrote, "It is in the character of very few men to honor without envy a friend who has prospered." The truth of that endures. What does your friend say when you get a promotion? I hope you have friends who say, "Isn't it wonderful!" But there are always those who are not cheering, especially if they were contending for the promotion. Max Beerbohm, in our own century, has said, "The dullard's envy of brilliant men is always assuaged by the suspicion that they will come to a bad end." Philip James Bailey gives the subject a theological interpretation, "Envy's coal comes hissing hot from hell."

Covetousness is the stuff of fairy tales as well. Remember the story of the fisherman who caught a magic fish. "Spare my life," pleads the fish, "and I'll give you three wishes." The fisherman agrees and goes home to tell his wife about this offer. "Tell the fish I want a bigger house," says she. The magic fish does her bidding, but she's not satisfied. She keeps wishing for ever-bigger houses. Speaking of his wife to the fish, the fisherman called her, "the bane of my life" and she was that, in spades. As children, we couldn't believe her greed. Then we grew up and turned into the fisherman's wife. We envy and covet and are caught in ever-escalating desires for more and bigger and better.

Two hundred years ago, Benjamin Franklin said, "The eyes of other people are the eyes that ruin us. If all but myself were blind, I should want neither fine clothes, fine houses, nor fine furniture." This constant measuring of ourselves against our neighbor is at the heart of covetousness. The whole point of living in a bigger or better house, driving a bigger and newer car, wearing more expensive clothes, is to impress and surpass my neighbor. If he or she doesn't even notice, all is for nothing. It boils down to this. I covet you to covet me. That's the sickness of our materialistic society.

Coveting is actually a kind of idolatry. Our well-being depends on getting something we don't have—that wife or that husband, that position or that money, that house or that car. Jesus said, "I came that you might have joy, that my joy might be in you . . ." We are willing to settle for a lot less. Rather than joy, we want what our neighbor has. We want what our friends have. We are as deserving as they are. We are putting all those things we covet in the place of the living God, who will be our joy and supply our needs. The twenty-third Psalm is a universal favorite, and in it we find amazing promises. The Lord is a shepherd who takes care of us, who feeds and comforts us, who leads us to rest in green pastures. With that kind of a shepherd, we need not covet. Our needs will be taken care of.

In the nineteenth chapter of Matthew's gospel, we read the account of Jesus' conversation with the rich young ruler. He is advised to sell his possessions and join the disciples, but his great wealth prevented him from doing so. The incident prompted Peter to ask about his own situation and that of his comrades. "We have left everything to follow you," he reminds Jesus; and he goes on to say, in effect, "What's in it for us?" In reply, Jesus makes that incredible statement that everyone who has left "houses or brothers or sisters or fathers or mothers or children or fields for my sake will receive a hundred times as much, and will inherit eternal life."

I know I am not alone in experiencing the reliability of that promise. I am an only child, and yet God has provided me with beloved brothers and sisters in the faith, with nurturing mothers and fathers, with rewarding children, and not just my own three. Even houses and lands have been placed at my disposal at crucial times when they were needed. Our God has no unpaid debts in this life or the next. We can depend on Him, and that ought to free us from the sin of covetousness.

There are at least three effective strategies we can use as we try to obey this tenth commandment. First, we can claim that whatever we have now is enough. Other people's possessions will not bring us happiness. Further, my lack of this world's goods, even my misfortunes, cannot take away my joy. A statement made by Ted Kennedy, Jr., moved me profoundly. "Losing a leg was actually a positive aspect of my life," he said. "It made me realize who I am, and in facing up to that challenge, I think that any challenge that comes my way I'll be able to deal with." It would be understandable for this prince of privilege who has lost his leg to cancer to covet the healthy legs of any of his peers. He could spend the rest of his life bemoaning his fate. "Why me? It's rotten." He didn't and wouldn't choose to lose a leg, but, having lost it, he has learned positive lessons that will change his life.

We close the door on all our covetousness when we can say, "God, what I have is enough." Paul writes in his letter to the Philippians, "I have learned the secret of being content in any and every situation, whether well fed or hungry, whether living in plenty or in want." Throughout his ministry, Paul was often hungry and in want, beaten, persecuted, and jailed, but he also had brothers, sisters, mothers, fathers, children, houses, lands a hundred-fold, scattered throughout all of Europe and Asia. We may not have endured the extremes Paul speaks of, but life is a sine wave for all of us. We can't escape the ups and downs. Even in the down times, we can believe God has provided for us.

There is a second helpful strategy in combating this covetousness we are all so prone to. Claim the long view of life. See the horizon. Psychologists tell us that delayed gratification is a sign of maturity. I don't have to have all my desires met right now. Further, I need not insist they be met with somebody else's wife or husband, job or possessions. As God's child, I have a history. I am on a pilgrimage. I can wait for fulfillment because I have the Lord's promise that all my needs will be met a hundred-fold and beyond. Don't give up that horizon, that long view, by insisting on having something which is not yours.

As I visit patients in nursing homes, I find those people who have lost their mental capacity far more pathetic than those with physical disabilities. They have no past and no future. They live in the now of the next meal or the next bowel movement. They have forgotten who they were, the battles won or lost, the loved ones living or dead. There is nothing ahead. There is only this day, this hour. But, there are people with all their faculties who live that way outside the nursing homes, unaware of any distant horizons, and that is the saddest state of all. God has promised us a future—family, houses, lands, in this life and eternal life beyond that.

Finally, I suggest positive addiction as a means of keeping this last commandment. We are compulsive people. We are familiar with negative addictions to dope or booze, but coveting can be an addiction as well. The good news is that we can replace a harmful addiction with a benign one. The Bible suggests we covet righteousness. Jacob coveted God's blessing. He was willing to lie and cheat and steal to get that blessing. As reprehensible as that is, it's better than being honest and upright and utterly indifferent about God's blessing. Throughout the Old and New Testaments, God has honored those who coveted His blessing and presence in their lives. Some of us have had some success in replacing an addiction to overeating with a commitment to healthy exercise and wise nutrition. That same principle will work for us in this area.

Covet righteousness, and all those other things we covet will lose their charm. Keep your eyes on the Jesus who made this extraordinary promise. He gives us all we need in this life by a hundred-fold and eternal life as well.

Part III. GOD THE HIDDEN HELPER

19. The Back Side of God

While Moses was on the mountain conversing with God and recording these commandments we have been talking about, some strange events were taking place in the camp of the Israelites. Their leader had been absent so long that they had given up on him. In their most flagrant act of disloyalty and disobedience, they ask Aaron to make them idols to worship. They are disillusioned with Moses and ready to abandon their living, delivering God.

It is a disheartening episode, and yet in it we find the very essence of the biblical message. It is the age-old story repeated over and over in the Old Testament of a people's disobedience and sin and of God's unmerited grace and favor and His delivering intervention.

One of the most surprising aspects of the story is that Aaron, Moses' coleader, spokesman, and family member, acceded to the request for an idol. The people contributed all their gold ornaments, and we read that he took what they handed him and made it into an idol cast in the shape of a calf, "fashioning it with a tool." Further, Aaron built an altar for this golden god and proclaimed the next day a feast day. "And they rose up early on the morrow, and offered burnt offerings and brought peace offerings, and the people sat down to eat and drink and indulge in revelry."

Meanwhile, Moses was warned by God of what was happening and directed to return immediately. His reaction is predictable: "When Moses approached the camp and saw the calf and the dancing, his anger burned, and he threw the tables out of his hands breaking them to pieces at the foot of the mountain. And he took the calf they had made and burned it in the fire . . ." He holds Aaron responsible and demands to know how this came about. His brother's excuse is a lame one. Aaron begins with a disclaimer, "You know how prone these people are to evil," and he ends by denying responsibility, ". . . they gave me the gold and I threw it into the fire, and out came this calf."

If all we had of the Old Testament was this one chapter, we would, nevertheless, have a clear picture of the human condition and predicament through the ages. It provides a piercing insight into the nature of sin, then and now. Basically, sin is nothing more or less than separation from God. Hell is not necessarily a place of punishment and eternal fires. Hell is that place where we are cut off from that Person who made us and loves us, the source of all life and joy. The temperature, hot or cold, is incidental. Sin, then, is anything that cuts us off from that source of life, from God's presence and love.

Aaron's sin, primarily, is that he bends to the will of the people. He gives them what they want—a god with a face, a god who is movable, a god of substance, above all, a god they can control. At last they have what they want, and they begin to celebrate wildly. Moses' anger, a reflection of God's anger, is awesome. He breaks the tablets, God's gift of the law, and takes his brother to task.

We recognize in Aaron's reply the self-deceit and injured innocence to which we are all so prone, and, to that end, we will paraphrase it a little. "Now wait a minute, little brother. Are you going to believe what you see, or do you want the truth? You know how evil these people are here. They came to me and said they needed a god, that this fellow Moses was gone and probably dead by now. They demanded a god they could see and handle and worship. They brought me their rings and I threw them in the fire, and out came this golden calf. I couldn't be more surprised. Don't blame me. My part in all this was minimal." It was the ultimate hypocrisy. Moses meted out an inordinately cruel punishment, or so it seems to us. He rallied those still faithful to the Lord, the Levites. They strapped on swords and cut down three thousand of the revelers, who are by this time running wild through the camp. It's a horrifying tale of bloody carnage with brother slaying brother.

Still, in the wake of all that, Moses has not given up on his people. The very next day he intercedes for them. "But, now, please, forgive their sins, but if not, blot me out of the book you have written." It is a moving petition. If God won't forgive His people, then He must cast Moses aside as well. In the New Testament, we find the apostle Paul in his letter to the Romans trying to make a similar exchange for his unbelieving Jewish brothers. "For I could wish that I myself were cursed and cut off from Christ for the sake of my brothers, those of my own race" (Romans 9:3).

The Israelites sinned grossly, and yet God continued to be their present and delivering God. As we said, this strange story paints one of Scripture's most clinical definitions of sin. First of all, sin is ingratitude. Ingratitude is, I suppose, one of the most despicable human traits. We abhore ungrateful children who receive nurture and love from their parents and grow up to neglect and ignore them. There are ungrateful friends who will take all we can give and disappear when we need them most.

All those kinds of stories pale compared to the attitude of the Israelites. God has brought them out of Egypt with a series of miracles. Plagues and disasters were visited upon the Egyptians. The Red Sea was opened, to enable them to cross and closed again to drown the entire Egyptian army. In the barren wilderness, food was provided, manna to eat daily. Bitter water was turned sweet. The law was to be the supreme gift. But they were too restless to wait for it. They grumbled, and the gist of their grumbling was, "What has God done for us lately?"

It is a human failing. I've been there, and I'll bet you have. What has God done for me lately? If sin is ingratitude, then we are all guilty. Our ingratitude tends to take a "why me?" slant. "I've been a faithful believer all these years, and now I'm out of a job. Doesn't God care about me?" Or, "I've been a Christian all my life, why did I get cancer?" My mother, who was one of

God's most valiant and faithful servants, felt at the end that God had let her down. She wanted to die. She wanted to go home. She didn't want to be old and frail and helpless. God had provided for her all through her life, but when He wouldn't bring her home on her timetable, she was good and mad at Him. To some degree, we all have that tendency. When something bad happens we question the value of our faith and the reality of God's love.

Isaac B. Singer, Nobel Prize winner, is one of my favorite authors. His short story "A Nest Egg Paradise," is about a pious Jew named Mendel who falls victim to sexual lust and has an affair with his sister-in-law. Remorseful, he seeks out the rabbi in the next village and confesses. "I have forfeited my share in the world to come," he says. To his surprise, the rabbi congratulates him. "The master of the universe has plenty of paid servants, but of those who would serve him for nothing, he has hardly any at all." Doesn't that put all this in perspective? We are not working for rewards. We are not even working for salvation. I have said on more than one occasion that, if there were no eternal life, no homecoming, the Christian life would all be worth it anyway, just for the excitement, the relationships, the joy of life in the Kingdom right now. That life is marked by a spirit of thanksgiving and gratitude.

Second, sin is self-centeredness. "I'll do it my way." Wife, husband, children, friends, church, job, all revolve around me. I am at the center. The Israelites wanted a god of substance. That kind of god is at your disposal. He goes where you want. He does what you want. Their delivering God was simply a pillar of fire by night and a pillar of cloud by day. He moves when and as He chooses. His spokesman was Moses, a charismatic leader, who seemed unreliable. Who wants that? They wanted something tangible and dependable and programmable, and that is exactly what the golden calf was meant to be.

The Egyptians, the Assyrians, in fact all their surrounding neighbors, had manmade gods. The Israelites wanted what their neighbors had. They were tired of being different. We can identify with that. Christians are set apart to be a peculiar people, a salt, a leaven, obedient to God. Christians are not necessarily nice people who don't drink or swear, lust or gossip. If you don't do any of those things, I commend you. But it is not your goodness and niceness that makes you a Christian. We are those who say, "Not my will, Lord, but Thy will be done." That makes us a different people.

In speaking of the Israelites to Moses, God called them a stiff-necked people. That's a farming term and has nothing to do with sore neck muscles. Oxen and horses out working in the field have a rope around their necks, which enables their master to direct and guide them. Occasionally, the animal won't bend, in spite of repeated tugging on the rope. They can't be moved. They just go their own way. That's a stiff-necked animal. The Israelites fit that description, and we often do. In spite of repeated tugs, we choose our will, not His. That was the beauty of a golden calf god. It would go their way. Incidentally, the golden calf was actually a bull, not a calf. The English translation is in error. The idol was a full-grown bull, which is exactly what the Egyptians and the Assyrians worshiped—a lot of bull.

Aaron gave the people what they wanted. His kind of leadership was a stark contrast to that of Moses, the prophet. Moses was dedicated to hearing and understanding God's will and then passing those instructions on to the people. Aaron, on the other hand, was merely a barometer. He read the climate of the crowd. "What do you all want? I'm your man. Let's take a poll. Whatever the majority wants, I'll get it for you."

We are still given the choice of those two kinds of leadership. We can elect those people to state and national office who will simply make sure we get our share of tax dollars and guarantee employment for our citizens. Occasionally, a Moses gets elected, somebody who will vote his or her conscience under God. Too often, we want somebody we can control, who will act consistently to further our own parochial interests. Those people without price, who stand for justice and truth whatever the majority want, are rare.

One of the strengths of my own Presbyterian tradition is in the fact that the pulpit belongs solely to the pastor, not to the congregation or to the church officers. Those invited to preach do so at the pastor's discretion and, furthermore, he can say or do whatever he wants to, as long as it's not heresy. From time to time, people leave our church because they don't agree with what is being said in the pulpit, politically, ethically, or theologically. Nevertheless, the message is mine to proclaim, and I am free to preach whatever God lays on my heart. I need not take a poll and then offer a composite of what we all believe as a congregation. Prophetic preaching is protected and cherished in our Presbyterian system.

We find a third definition of sin emerging from this golden calf story. Sin is pretended innocence, and that is at the heart of a good many of our problems. Adam and Eve sinned when God laid down just one rule. Confronted by God about his disobedience, Adam passed the buck. "It's not my fault. The woman whom you gave me made me do this." Eve was quick to protest that it's not her fault. The serpent, the shining one, made her do it. Neither is guilty, neither repents, neither is forgiven. Pretended innocence is perhaps the thing that most separates us not just from God but from each other. It is the most tragic kind of sin.

The New Testament mentions the unforgivable sin, and there is much speculation about what that might be. We are told that it is the sin against the Holy Spirit. The Holy Spirit has two important functions. The first is to convict us of sin. God has given us clear laws about how to live. We disregard them, we equivocate and say, "Nobody follows those rules any more. Times have changed." But, as we move away from those ten channel markers, the Spirit is at work prodding our conscience. The Spirit makes it clear that we are out of the channel. The second function of the Spirit is to remind us of God's grace. He loves us. We can come home again. Our natural response to our own misdeeds is the one that Aaron makes. "It wasn't my fault. I just threw in this gold, and out came a calf." By our pretended innocence, we put ourselves beyond God's grace. We cannot be forgiven unless we confess we have been wrong.

Our human relationships break down when we are unable to forgive each other. I have failed family and friends and I have been failed on occasion. It is hard to resist a genuine apology under those circumstances. "Dad, brother, husband, I hurt you. I offended you. I'm sorry." We all love to forgive. It makes us feel magnanimous and at peace with ourselves. Relationships break down when nobody is willing to be wrong. We spend our lives proving our innocence. "Well, under the circumstances . . ." "All I said was . . ."

We have so many ways to rationalize our misdeeds. I had to steal—my company does not pay me enough. I had to have an affair—my spouse is frigid. I had to cheat in class—everyone does. I have a nasty disposition because my mother didn't love me. I'm an alcoholic because my parents are alcoholics. I'm overweight because of my glands. I take sleeping pills because I am so lonely and misunderstood. I take drugs because of all the stress in my life.

We are all innocent. We are the victims of circumstances and yet our only hope with God or man is to confess we are guilty. We are all sinners. We need a Savior who offers us forgiveness and new life. If and when we are convicted by the Holy Spirit of our wrongdoing, we have an opportunity for that second chance and a third and beyond.

A. J. Cronin, the novelist, was also a doctor. His first assignment was to a Welsh town where he performed his first surgery on a little girl with a serious case of diphtheria. He did a tracheotomy and her condition improved, though it was still critical. After the operation, he told the nineteen-year-old nurse on duty, "I'm going to try to get some sleep. When this tube clogs up, take it out immediately and clean it. Then, come and get me."

Within hours, the tube did clog up. The nurse panicked and ran for the doctor, but by the time Cronin arrived, the girl was dead. He was furious, and the very next day wrote a letter recommending that her nursing license be revoked. He called her in and read it to her. The nurse, close to tears, pleaded for a second chance, but he was unrelenting. However, her words haunted Cronin all night. He awoke in the morning remembering that that's exactly what he had once said to Jesus. "Give me a second chance." The nurse was given a second chance and went on to become the superintendent of the biggest children's hospital in Britain.

The Israelites were given a second chance. In the midst of their sins of ingratitude, self-centeredness, and pretended innocence, they had an intercessor, Moses. He reminds God of His own nature—that He is a forgiving God. Forgiveness is costly always. If you have forgiven a spouse's infidelity, you have paid a great price, more than most are willing to pay. If you have forgiven a parent who abused you, emotionally or even sexually, you have paid a great price. If, like the Prodigal's father, you have forgiven a child who has disappointed you and deserted you, you have paid a great price. If you have forgiven a friend who has betrayed you, one whom you have given your trust and your heart, you have paid a price. If you have had any of those experiences, you have a special understanding of the cross. Forgiveness, human or divine, is costly. God has paid the price. We are loved because we are loved, not because we are good, not because we are deserving. We are loved because it is God's nature to love.

Nevertheless, God was offended enough with the Israelites to institute new rules. He would, in the future, talk to Moses in a tent of meeting, outside the camp. There Moses met with God and they communed. Whenever Moses went into the tent of meeting, every man stood at his tent door with his head uncovered and watched. They were reassured that God had not abandoned them. He was talking even now to Moses.

At one of those sessions, Moses asked a favor. "I pray Thee, show me Thy glory." The Lord agrees, but with a condition. "You cannot see my face, for man shall not see me and live . . . and while my glory passes by, I will put you in a cleft of the rock, and I will cover you with my hand until I have passed by. Then I will take away my hand and you shall see my back, but my face shall not be seen." There are some wonderful old hymns which are based on this story. "He Hideth my Soul in the Cleft of the Rock" is one; "Rock of Ages," everybody's mother's favorite, is another. Moses will die if he sees God's face. He is to stand in the opening of the rock over which God will place His hand while "all my glory passes by." Afterward, God will take His hand away and Moses will see His back.

Is it possible that in those places where God is most present, His face is hidden from us? The theology of suffering is attributed to Martin Luther, and it ties in directly with this very idea. You may remember that at the early part of our century there was a great revival of liberalism. The message was that the church would build a new, peaceful, wonderful world—not the Kingdom of God, but a just society. That dream died with the advent, first of all, of World War I and then World War II with millions of people killed and countless cities destroyed.

In the ashes of that dream, Luther was rediscovered. Luther's interpretation of the text, "The just shall live by faith" sparked reformation, but, he had also made a profound observation in answer to the question which every generation asks. "Where is God most present in the world?" "At the cross where His Son died," was Luther's answer. Where there is suffering in the world, that is where God is most present. But the problem is that while God may be most present there, we cannot see His face in the midst of our suffering. We cry, "Where is God?" Only later do we see, in retrospect, that He was indeed there. We see the back side of God and know He was surely among us.

You have been there. Only after the tragedy were you overwhelmed with the sense of God's presence. I have been there. I look back on three of the darkest years of my life and realize I have never known God's grace more acutely than I did throughout that suffering. Imagine for a moment that you were present at Calvary and witnessed that scene at Golgotha. It was a terrible moment from any point of view. Even the Roman soldiers would be saying, "This man was innocent. His trial was a mockery. This is a pointless miscarriage of justice." If you were there as a believer, you would be desolate. "Don't they realize this is the Son of God? This is the worst moment in the history of the world." Just three days later, after the resurrection, you would have a new understanding of it all. You would say that God was never more present than on that hill in Calvary. Faith, then, is believing even when you are going through life's inevitable dark valleys that God is present. Only later will you see His back.

A young woman who sang in our church's choir went through a heartbreaking experience a few years ago. She was a single parent with one little boy, Joshua. One sunny afternoon, Josh was riding his bicycle and was struck by a car and went into a coma. He remained in that state for almost three months. The family of faith surrounded this single parent, Kathy. They brought in meals and visited Joshua and prayed unceasingly for him. Joshua's death, after those agonizing months, was hard to accept. The funeral was a moving homecoming, and church friends were there in great numbers.

Eventually, Kathy moved back to Illinois to live near her parents; but she has since written me, "Bruce, those three months were the most amazing months of my life. I have never known the presence of God more than I did in those days." It is hard to explain when the worst is happening that God is there. But He is, and He will reveal His presence later. If only we could draw on that certainty in advance.

Well, Moses saw God's glory, after He passed; but the Exodus story doesn't end there. Actually, the concluding events seem almost anticlimactic. The two tablets are again given to Moses, and this time they remain intact. God renews His covenant with the Israelites, and the last six chapters of this second Old Testament book describe the construction of the Tabernacle and provide a detailed discussion of the theology of worship. The

Tabernacle erected in the camp was tangible evidence that God, their delivering God, had come to dwell with His people.

It is a happy ending to this long, dramatic tale of deliverance, and that in itself is astonishing. We begin to have some deeper understanding of God's nature. Humanly speaking, that golden calf ought to have been the last straw. God had every reason to give up on the Israelites, abandon them. But the covenant made with Abraham, Isaac and Jacob was still binding. Their descendants, petty and grumbling, disobedient, and disloyal, were still His people.

The great, good news for God's people today is that He is in our midst. He is not in a cloud, or a pillar of fire. He is not in a Tabernacle, or a temple. The Holy Spirit of our delivering God is in the hearts of His faithful people. We may turn to other idols temporarily, but His love and forgiveness are certain. We may feel abandoned, cut off by illness, loss, misfortune, but help is always on the way. We are promised not just deliverance, but the love and presence of the Deliverer.